ILLUSTRATING
CHILDREN'S BOOKS
History — Technique — Production

ALICE AND MARTIN PROVENSEN
The Golden Treasury of Myths and Legends
Golden Press

ILLUSTRATING CHILDREN'S BOOKS

History — Technique — Production

HENRY C. PITZ

New York
Watson-Guptill Publications

To Norman Kent,
who persuaded me to do this book.

Second Printing 1965
Third Printing 1967
Copyright ©1963 by Watson-Guptill Publications, Inc.
New York, New York

PREFACE

There is certainly temerity in attempting to cover a very large subject in less than two hundred pages. But I do not think it has been the temerity of ignorance. I knew what I was getting into. But the making of pictures for children's books, while scarcely a neglected subject, is certainly rather sparsely documented. Surprisingly little has been written about its past and present, its history, and its techniques of production. There is room for many research projects on the earlier children's books, and today's flood of material is in such volume as to frighten off documentation and evaluation.

So here is an attempt to outline the development of the children's picture book; to bring it up to the impetuous present; to evaluate the present moment; and then to describe in simple form the practices and techniques that bring the artist's pictorial ideas into finished form on the printed book page.

Any author who pauses upon the completion of a book, reviews its sources and enumerates all the helping hands that have put him in possession of his material, must be astounded at the ever-widening network of his obligations. I can see my obligations stretching back to my earliest childhood: the longer I look, the more I rediscover. Like all other authors, I must limit my public thanks and mention only those most immediately and recently concerned.

First, Norman Kent, who persuaded me to write this book and who has helped me with illustrative material. Then the many editors, who entrusted me with so many manuscripts to illustrate over the years: Louise Seaman Bechtel, William Fayal Clark, Scotson Clark, Bertha Gunterman, Lillian Bragdon, Diana Klemin, John Martin and many others. Also the many editors who have brought recent work to my attention and supplied me with copious material, much more than I have been able to use: Alice Dalgleish, Margaret McIlderry, Virginia Fowler and Diana Klemin. David Bland of Faber and Faber has brought much recent British work to my attention and generously loaded me down with books. My friend, Percy H. Muir, has unconsciously helped me in many a conversation and letter and has allowed me to plunder his book, *English Children's Books,* for quotations.

As in the case of a previous book of mine, Lucille Ogle has been very generous of her time and knowledge, particularly in assembling the material for color reproduction. Gerry De Mann has assisted in the preparation of the color section. Mary Knowles of the William Jeanes Memorial Library cheerfully and untiringly secured pertinent reference books from distant places. Both Carolyn Field and Grace M. Zahn of the Central Library, Philadelphia, have contributed help and ideas. William McCarthy of the Rosenbach Foundation has made available to me the foundation's extensive collection of American juvenile books.

I am indebted to my illustrator friends who have loaned me original drawings. Many publishers have permitted drawings to be used and these sources are credited under the reproductions. Finally, Donald Holden and Jules Perel have enthusiastically cheered me on and performed the expert task of editing and production. My wife has faithfully typed this manuscript (as she has the manuscripts of my previous books); has uncomplainingly corrected spelling and punctuation; and has made approving sounds from time to time. From year to year, the typing improves; the spelling changes, but doesn't improve.

Plymouth Meeting — Pennsylvania
Henry C. Pitz

CONTENTS

Preface 5

List of Illustrations 9

PART I. HISTORY
Chapter

1. Pictures for Childhood 13

2. The Earlier Books 19

3. England after 1800 31

4. Europe from 1800 on 51

5. America — The Earlier Years 61

6. Howard Pyle and the Brandywine Tradition 67

7. The American Accent 75

8. Toward the Present 79

9. Matters Ponderable and Imponderable 99

PART II. TECHNIQUE AND PRODUCTION

10. The Illustrator in the Children's World 105

> The Picturebook Age
> Learning to Read
> The Most Important Reading Age
> Towards Adulthood
> Observing Children

11. The Structure of the Book 135
The Book Jacket
The Casing
The End Papers
The Front Matter
The Body of the Book

12. Typography and Book Design 151

13. Methods of Reproduction 157
Relief
Intaglio
Planographic

14. Preparing Pictures for Reproduction 165
Bleeds
Sizes in Reproduction
Drawing for the Line Cut
Color Separations for Line Reproduction
Halftone Effects in Line
Drawing for Halftone

PART III. PROFESSIONAL PRACTICE

15. Handling an Assignment 187

16. Getting Work 193
Portfolio Presentation

17. The Field Today 197

Bibliography 204

Index 206

LIST OF ILLUSTRATIONS

Page

2 ALICE AND MARTIN PROVENSEN.
Golden Treasury of Myths and Legends
12 JEROME SNYDER. Umbrellas, Hats and Wheels
13 BETH KRUSH. Bobby and his Band
14 FEODOR ROJANKOVSKY. Over in the Meadow
15 JOSEPH LOW. Mother Goose Riddle Rhymes
16 REINER ZIMNIK. Drummers of Dreams
17 GUSTAF TENGGREN. Farm Stories
18 MARY SHEPARD. Mary Poppins
19 EDWARD SOREL. King Carlo of Capri
20 COMENIUS. Orbis Sensualium Pictus, 1658
21 Der Ritter Vom Turm, 1493
21 The Caxton "Easop," 1484
22 Topsel's History of Four-Footed Beasts, 1658
24 Queen Elizabeth
24 Sir Bevis of Hampton
24 True Tale of Robin Hood
24 Sir Richard Whittington
27 WILLIAM BLAKE. Songs of Innocence
and Experience
28 WILLIAM BLAKE. Songs of Innocence
and Experience
29 THOMAS BEWICK. White Line Wood Engravings
30 THOMAS BEWICK
31 GEORGE CRUIKSHANK. Modern Illustration
32 GEORGE CRUIKSHANK. Cinderella
33 JOHN LEECH. Pictures of Life and Character
34 ERNEST GRISET. National Nursery Rhymes
35 RICHARD DOYLE. Decorative Initial
35 J. B. ZWECKER. National Nursery Rhymes
35 ARTHUR BOYD HOUGHTON.
Dalziel's Arabian Nights
36 EDWARD LEAR. Nonsense Songs, Stories,
Botany and Alphabets
37 JOHN TENNIEL. Alice's Adventures
in Wonderland
37 EDWARD LEAR. Nonsense Songs, Stories,
Botany and Alphabets
39 WALTER CRANE. The First of May
40 KATE GREENAWAY. Sketch
40 RANDOLPH CALDECOTT. Author's Collection
41 WILLIAM NICHOLSON. An Alphabet
41 HUGH THOMSON. Pride and Prejudice
43 BEATRIX POTTER. Two Bad Mice
43 ARTHUR RACKHAM. Peer Gynt
44 EDMUND DULAC. The Real Princess
45 CLAUD LOVAT FRASER. Poems
45 GWEN RAVERAT. Bird Talisman
45 JOAN HASSALL. Our Village
46 ERNEST H. SHEPARD. The Wind in the Willows
46 EDWARD BAWDEN. Take The Broom
47 RONALD SEARLE. The Terror of St. Trinians
48 DENNIS WIRTH-MILLER and
RICHARD CHOPPING. Heads, Bodies and Legs
49 LEWITT-HIM. The Little Red Engine
Gets a Name
49 MAURICE WILSON. Zoo Animals
49 GRACE GABLER. A Child's Alphabet
50 PRISCILLA THORNYCROFT. Whiskers the Cat
51 LUDWIG RICHTER. Deutsche Art und Sitte
52 DR. HEINRICH HOFFMANN. Struwwelpeter
52 WILHELM BUSCH. Balduin Bahlamm
53 LUDWIG RICHTER. Fürs Haus
54 KAY NIELSEN. East of the Sun and
West of the Moon
54 HANS TEGNER
55 GUSTAVE DORE. Author's collection
56 JEAN DE BRUNHOFF. Babar books
57 M. BOUTET DE MONVEL. Jeanne D'Arc
57 EDY LEGRAND. Little Story of Lafayette
58 REINER ZIMNIK. Drummers of Dreams
59 JOHN BAUER. Bästa
60 JIRE TRNKA
61 Woodcut of Richard Mather
Earliest known American illustration
62 ALEXANDER ANDERSON. Wood Engraving
62 Page from children's A.B.C. distributed by
patent medicine firm
63 ALEXANDER ANDERSON. Wood Engravings
63 Typical Early Booklet for Children
64 WINSLOW HOMER. Our Young Folks
64 Title Page for Typical Children's Book Series
65 FELIX DARLEY. Preliminary Sketches
66 HOWARD PYLE. Harper's Young People
67 HOWARD PYLE. King Arthur and his Knights
69 HOWARD PYLE. King Arthur and his Knights
70 HOWARD PYLE. Harper's Young People
71 FRANK SCHOONOVER. Robinson Crusoe
71 N. C. WYETH. Black Arrow
72 JESSIE WILLCOX SMITH.
Child's Garden of Verses
73 EDWARD A. WILSON. Iron Men and
Wooden Ships
74 HOWARD PYLE. Harper's Young People
75 A. B. FROST. Uncle Remus
76 A. B. FROST. Uncle Remus
77 A. B. FROST. Uncle Remus
77 FREDERIC REMINGTON. Sketch
78 EDWARD W. KEMBLE. Author's collection
79 MAE GERHARD. Unpublished illustration
80 PALMER COX. The Brownies at Home
81 PALMER COX. The Brownies at Home
81 WALTER HARRISON CADY. The Happy Chaps
82 C. B. FALLS. A.B.C. Book
84 KATHERINE MILHOUS. With Bells On
84 EDWARD SHENTON. Best in Children's Books
84 SHEILAH BECKETT
85 BORIS ARTZYBASHEFF. Poor Shaydulla
85 VALENTI ANGELO. Golden Gate
85 JAMES DAUGHERTY. Knickerbocker's
History of New York
86 LYND WARD. The Canadian Story
89 DR. SEUSS. The Sneetches and Other Stories
89 HENRY C. PITZ. With Might and Main
91 FEODOR ROJANKOVSKY.
The Tall Mother Goose
91 GUSTAF TENGGREN. Tenggren's Story Book

92 NICOLAS MORDVINOFF.
Pepe Was the Saddest Bird
93 LEONARD WEISGARD
93 RICHARD FLOETHE. If I were Captain
94 MARCIA BROWN. Once a Mouse
94 LEONA PIERCE. Who Likes the Sun?
95 ANTONIO FRASCONI. The Snow and the Sun
96 J. P. MILLER. The Wonderful House
97 ROGER DUVOISIN. Veronica
99 REINER ZIMNIK. Drummers of Dreams
102 ERIK BLEGVAD. I'm Hiding
104 HILARY KNIGHT. Beloved Tales
105 MARY VILLAREJO. The Art Fair
111 HILARY KNIGHT. Beloved Tales
112 TIBOR GERGELY. A Day in the Jungle
113 TIBOR GERGELY. A Day in the Jungle
114 WALT DISNEY. Walt Disney's Story Land
115 WILLIAM DUGAN. Old Friends and
Lasting Favorites
116 J. P. MILLER. The Wonderful House
117 RICHARD SCARRY. Beloved Tales
118 MURRAY TINKLEMAN. Who Says Hoo?
119 LILIAN OBLIGADO. Beloved Tales
120 EDWARD SOREL. Gwendolyn the Miracle Hen
121 GUSTAF TENGGREN. Farm Stories
122-3 ALICE and MARTIN PROVENSEN.
The Golden Treasury of Myths and Legends
124 FEODOR ROJANKOVSKY.
The Tall Book of Mother Goose
125 FEODOR ROJANKOVSKY.
The Tall Book of Mother Goose
126 ELOISE WILKIN. Old Friends and
Lasting Favorites
126 GORDON LAITE. Beloved Tales
127 NICOLAS MORDVINOFF. Just So Stories
128 LOWELL HESS. Old Friends and
Lasting Favorites
129 MAE GERHARD. Old Friends and
Lasting Favorites
130 GORDON LAITE. Old Friends and
Lasting Favorites
131 ARTHUR SINGER. The Giant Golden Book
of Birds
132 RUDOLF FREUND. American Butterflies
and Moths
133 HARRY McNAUGHT. The Golden Book
of Science
134 MAE GERHARD. Old Friends and
Lasting Favorites
134 WILLIAM DUGAN. Old Friends and
Lasting Favorites
135 LEONARD WEISGARD. The Secret River
137 GERALD ROSE. Old Winkle and the Seagulls
139 LEONA PIERCE. Who Likes the Sun?
139 REMY CHARLIP. A Day of Winter
140 Structural diagram of a book
141 ROGER DUVOISIN. Veronica
142 MARCIA BROWN. Once a Mouse
142 DAHLOV IPCAR. Deep Sea Farm

142 JOSEPH LOW. Mother Goose Riddle Rhymes
143 WARREN CHAPPELL. The Sleeping Beauty
144 ALDREN WATSON. Fairy Tales of the
Grimm Brothers
144 MARCIA BROWN. Once a Mouse
145 BENI MONTRESOR. Mommies at Work
145 FEODOR ROJANKOVSKY. The Whirly Bird
145 HAROLD BERSON. A Pint of Judgment
147 HENRY C. PITZ. Hansel and Gretel
148 Double-page layouts
149 WARREN CHAPPELL. The Sleeping Beauty
149 ROBERT LAWSON. Rabbit Hill
150 MARVIN BILECK. Nobody's Birthday
151 JOSEPH LOW. Mother Goose Riddle Rhymes
153 A metal type slug
154 EDWARD BAWDEN. Tales of Troy and Greece
155 J. P. MILLER. A Wonderful House
155 PAUL RAND. Sparkle and Spin
157 ERIK BLEGVAD. I'm Hiding
159 Line plate diagram
161 Diagram of halftone dot pattern
162 Photogravure plate
163 The planographic surface
165 JEROME SNYDER. One Day in Ancient Rome
166 LEO POLITI. The Butterflies Come
167 Diagram of proportional enlarging
168 The drawing reduced
170 ROBERT FAWCETT. Young Hickory
171 Two-color reproduction. HENRY C. PITZ.
Best-In-Children's Books
172 Color Separation. Diagram of
transparent acetate overlay
175 Diagram of a light-box
176 Samples of Zip-a-tone, Craftint and BenDay
177 Shading tints and crayon
180 N. M. BODECKER. Sylvester
181 ADRIENNE SEGUR. Thumbelina Fun and Fancy
182 ERIK BLEGVAD. Where's Willie
182 The Three Process Colors
183 RUDOLF FREUND. American Butterflies
and Moths
184 W. W. DENSLOW. The Wonderful Wizard of Oz
186 A. BELIN. Fine Illustrated Books
187 GERALD ROSE. Old Winkle and the Seagulls
189 HENRY C. PITZ. The stages of an illustration.
20,000 Leagues Under the Sea
190 HENRY C. PITZ. Dummy drawing of
double-page endpapers
192 HENRY C. PITZ
193 EDWARD SOREL. King Carlo of Capri
197 MARCIA BROWN. Once a Mouse
198-9 BETH and JOSEPH KRUSH.
Coarse Gold Gulch
200 JAN LEWITT. The Vegatabull
200 JOSEPH LOW. Mother Goose Riddle Rhymes
201 GERALD ROSE. Old Winkle and the Seagulls
202 JANICE HOLLAND.
Christopher Goes to the Castle
202 LYLE JUSTIS. Unpublished illustration
203 HENRY C. PITZ

PART I. HISTORY

JEROME SNYDER
Umbrella, Hats and Wheels
Harcourt, Brace and Company

BETH KRUSH
Bobby and his Band
Harcourt, Brace and World

CHAPTER 1

Pictures for Childhood

ALL OVER THE WORLD THERE HAS BEEN a waxing appetite for pictures. It is a hunger that has been growing for decades in most countries, and is only partly satisfied by the mechanical marvels that print countless thousands of reproduced pictures. In America it seems to take its most acute form. Today the average American lives in a picture-saturated world. He walks streets lined with pictorial billboards, signs, and window displays. He looks at car cards as he rides on buses or trains. He buys pictures by the score when purchasing newspapers and magazines. There is his television screen and the nearby movie house. Pictures invade his home with every mail — innumerable advertising pieces and more magazines. He may have pictures on his walls, and even buy illustrated books and go to art exhibitions. He seems to enjoy all this, but hurriedly.

Usually he is unconscious of the monster mechanism he has caused to grow up to satisfy his hasty hungers. It is a mechanism of giant size and power, designed for headlong speed and sharpest efficiency. The modern presses are miracles. They print enormous editions of full color or black and white material at gasping speeds. They are run by skilled pressmen, who theoretically should be the equal of any in the world; but with the premium on speed and quantity, the higher levels of quality are seldom reached. Painstaking care and a high regard for craftsmanship are not characteristic of American printing.

13

FEODOR ROJANKOVSKY
Over in the Meadow
Harcourt, Brace and Company

14

When we focus on one large section of this vast world of publication, that of children's books, we find the same enormous expansion of demand and production. The young are being deluged with printed matter as never before; although it is more apparent in America, it is a world-wide condition. The literature for children has become so vast a body of work that it is difficult to survey. Every day adds to the bulk of production and a small army attends to its demands.

The industry has built up its own interlocking mechanism of specialists: authors, editors, illustrators, designers, production men, advertisers, sales personnel, librarians, critics, and other talents. Numerous organizations, boards, and committees have been formed to deal with its problems. What was once a haphazard delight is now a highly organized operation, at times threatening to lose sight of its primary purpose.

Its record is impressive, however. Children are being offered not only the largest amount of text and picture material the world has ever seen, but the material is amazing in its variety of content and format and in the average high level of its accomplishment. Not only is the annual output of children's books remarkable in its sheer numbers, but the array of titles is exciting and bewildering in its brightness, smartness, its design-skill and its fertility of invention. It is a gay array, stimulating the eye and inviting the hand and eye to open and examine the contents. The contents range from mediocre to excellent, but the average is high. There is great variety, much information conveyed with considerable skill, a lively bounce to most of the prose, and more than a little imagination. There are few texts that will last over the years but that probably would be asking too much. For books that are to last for a reading or two, the conditions are satisfied hundreds of times a year and if, in America, the addiction to obsolescence has not left this field untouched, there is a hard core of solid, craftsmanlike work studded with occasional gems that will sparkle for awhile.

The achievements of this field, its present-day bustle, and its promise of a waxing future have attracted a large body of eager and

JOSEPH LOW
Mother Goose Riddle Rhymes
Harcourt, Brace and Company

gifted men and women; and every year will undoubtedly bring a fresh company of recruits. The field needs in its recruits not only numbers but talent, not only romantic enthusiasm but endurance, not only opportunism but dedication.

The illustrator, picturemaker, and designer play a crucial part. They are figures of importance, working in an important sector of modern activity. Many of the important artists in the field have made a lifetime commitment to it. The field offers little to the chance opportunist, but it can offer a lifetime of satisfaction to the gifted and devoted.

This type of illustration is very hospitable to fresh talent; it has a certain weakness for mere novelty; it is susceptible to the ebb and flow of its own fashions; but association with the eternal awakening wonder of the child's mind preserves it from most of the tawdriness of the adult world.

The young person with illustrative gifts who feels any attraction toward this field should invest some time and effort in exploration. First, he should examine what is being done currently; second, he should explore the past, for the children's book illustrator of today is the child of his artistic ancestors; and, third, he should explore himself. The final key question to the last exploration is not "what can it do for me?" but "what can I do for it?"

REINER ZIMNIK
Drummers of Dreams
Faber and Faber

16

GUSTAF TENGGREN
Farm Stories
Simon and Schuster

17

MARY SHEPARD
Mary Poppins
Harcourt, Brace and World

18

EDWARD SOREL
King Carlo of Capri
Harcourt, Brace and Company

CHAPTER **2**

The Earlier Books

THE BOOKS OF CHILDHOOD are so much a part of our lives
that if we think of a time when there were none, we might be inclined to
go as far back as our cave-dwelling ancestors. The presence of books
as an accepted part of the average child's life is a fairly recent thing,
and as we trace back in history, the evidence of the existence of these
books thins out rapidly and soon we look hopefully for an occasional
guidepost. The literature on children's books is hardly scanty, but many
of its territories have been insufficiently explored. It is still an uncrowded
field for the scholar and historian.

Many discussions of the origin of the children's illustrated book
begin with Bishop Comenius (1592-1670). Comenius was a remarkable
man who had far-seeing ideas about making knowledge attractive to
young minds. Disgusted with the pedantic instruction of his day, he
instituted the idea of teaching language through pictures. He compiled
a book which appears to be one of the first children's picture books
of which we have evidence. This, *Orbis sensualium pictus*, was printed
in Nuremberg in 1658 and, shortly after, was translated into *Visible
World—for the Use of Young Latin Scholars,* for the first English
edition. It remained in print for more than a century. One often quoted
sentence of Comenius, "Pictures are the most intelligible books that
children can look upon," is certainly an age-old truth which has lost
none of its lustre. Comenius has usually been treated as a solitary

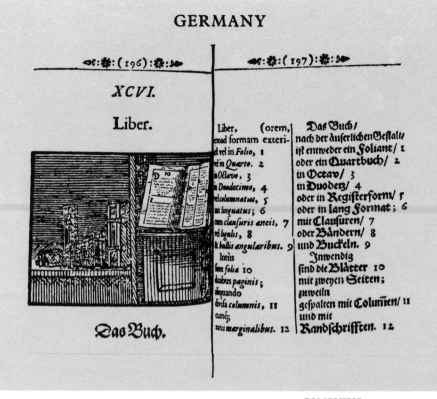

COMENIUS
Orbis sensualium pictus. 1658

enlightened figure in the development of children's education; but it might be fair to assume that while his teachings have survived the vicissitudes of history, others may have been obliterated by them.

Books with pictures for children were printed long before Comenius' textbook. There is *Der Ritter vom Turn,* printed with woodcuts in Switzerland in 1493; and Caxton in England, after printing several unillustrated books for children, produced an illustrated *Aesop* in 1484. For centuries there had been bestiaries used by the teaching monks but these, with their hand-illuminated pictures, were the work of scribes, and children could not hope to possess them.

In the seventeenth century there was scanty pictorial fare for the child. There was an ambitious volume of 1665, an *Aesop's Fables,*

DER RITTER VOM TURM
Printed in Switzerland, 1493

THE CAXTON "EASOP" *1484*
Part of page showing woodcut with type

ranne in to the forest / And whanne the wyld beestes sawe
hym come / they were so ferdfull that they alle beganne to flee /
For they wend / that it had be the lyon / And the mayster of
the asse serched and soughte his asse in every place al aboute
And as he had soughte longe / he thought that he wold go in
to the forest for to see yf his asse were there / And as soone as

THE
HISTORY
OF
Four-Footed Beasts.

The *ANTALOPE*.

THE *Antalope* called in Latin *Calopus*, and of the Grecians *Analopos*, or *Apiolos*: of this beast there is no mention made among the Ancient Writers, except *Suidas*, and the Epistle of *Alexander* to *Aristotle*, interpreted by *Cornelius Nepotius*. They are bred in *India* and *Syria*, neer the Countrey of River *Euphrates*, and delight much to drink of the cold water thereof: Their breed, body is like the body of a *Roe*, and they have horns growing forth of the crown of their head, which are very long and sharp; so that *Alexander* affirmed they pierced through the shields of his Souldiers, and fought with them very irefully: at which time his company slew as he travelled to *India*, eight thousand five hundred and fifty; which great slaughter may be the occasion why they are so rare, and seldom seen to this day, because thereby the breeders and means of their continuance (which consisted in their multitude) were weakned and destroyed. Their horns are great and made like a saw, and they with them can cut asunder the branches of Osier or small trees, whereby it cometh to passe that many times their necks are taken in the twists of the falling boughs, whereat the Beast with repining cry, bewrayeth himself to the Hunters, and so is taken. The virtues of this Beast is unknown, and therefore *Suidas* saith, an *Antalope* is but good in part.

TOPSEL
"History of Four-Footed Beasts," 1658

engraved by Hollar, Stoops, and Barlow. Wenzel Hollar was a very accomplished Bohemian etcher who had come to live in England. Francis Barlow may be called England's first illustrator, an artist of great endowments. These men produced a very handsome volume, but one so sumptuous that it was not apt to be put in children's hands except on special occasions. More likely to be regularly read by them was Crouch's *The Young Man's Calling* of 1678, with its successive revisions and reprintings. This was a pirating of Puritan texts with no intrusion of a lighthearted note, but the Calvinists knew the value of pictures as long as they served their own creed.

The Puritans were assiduous in the education of their young and published many books for them, but grimness runs through every one. The best of them, a classic, was Bunyan's *Pilgrim's Progress.* It was not intended for the young but they adopted it, as they have done so often with adult texts—and no wonder, for the Calvinist trappings thinly disguised a gripping adventure tale.

Much more widespread were the cheap chapbooks hawked by peddlers or chapmen throughout Britain. They may not have been intended directly for children, but inevitably they came under children's eyes. All the old heroes and heroines of legends and fairy tales were written about in them, together with gory happenings from history; and there were always some crude woodcuts. These chapbooks were cheaply and carelessly made, produced for those with little money and little or no education, but even the illiterate could gape at the crude pictures. Many thousands were sold, but their flimsiness and the fact that they passed from hand to hand prevented many from surviving to our day.

Not only the chapbook cuts but almost all of the pictures in early books look strange to us. We feel long removed from them, for our eyes have adjusted themselves to a different vocabulary of forms. Our sophistication may make us forget that one object of the picture is to set the imagination in motion. In the children of earlier days, the very sharpness of their hunger must have shown them things in those old cuts that are invisible to our sated twentieth century eyes.

Gradually the chapbooks gained respectability as more worthy publishers became interested in them and they became accepted as a suitable form for juveniles. By the early years of the eighteenth century there seems to have been an increasing awareness of the child public

QUEEN ELIZABETH
*From a chapbook
printed by J. White of Newcastle*

TRUE TALE OF ROBIN HOOD

SIR BEVIS OF HAMPTON

SIR RICHARD WHITTINGTON

These are typical specimens of woodcut illustrations printed in early chapbooks. These flimsy books were made to sell for a few pennies, and although produced by the thousands, relatively few have survived because of their shoddy materials and excessive handling. To us, nourished on richer and more varied pictorial fare, their principal appeal is quaintness but to seventeenth and eighteenth century children they must have opened windows upon strange and fascinating worlds.

and more attempts to cater to it. This is a period of conjecture, for little tangible evidence has survived, but as Percy Muir points out in his *English Children's Books*, children's books are one of the most ephemeral of all forms of printed matter. The cheap materials used in their production and the rigorous treatment they must withstand shorten their existence. In earlier times, when children's books were scarce, they were passed from hand to hand even more frequently than they do now, and many titles have probably entirely perished. This robs the historian of much of the original material on which to base his survey, and may lead to the dangerous assumption that what no longer survives never existed at all. " 'Few and far' indeed are the extant remnants of the period before John Newbery; and hence arose the unquestionably false assumption that until he came upon the scene no proper provision was made for children at all; and that with the publication, in 1744, of his *Little Pretty Pocket Book,* the scene was changed in the twinkling of an eye. This is a greatly oversimplified picture of the true situation."

Percy Muir goes on to trace the predecessors of Newbery (1713-1767) and shows him as less of an isolated figure than commonly supposed. He is still a landmark, however, and the commercial astuteness that enabled him to publish a long list of little books for children that accurately gauged the taste of the times, made him prosperous. Newbery's success demonstrated that here was a business that had untold possibilities.

Popularity of children's books soon became apparent throughout Europe and America. A German schoolmaster had this to say in 1787: "No other form of literary manufactory is so active as bookmaking for young people of all grades and classes. Every Leipzig Summer and Winter Fair throws up a countless number of books of this kind like a flooding tide. And see how young and old rush to buy—there are few pearls and little amber, but much mud, and, at the best, painted snail-shells. They take all kinds of names and forms; almanacs for children, newspapers for children, journals for children, dramas for children, geography for children, history for children, physics for children, logic for children, catechisms for children, travels for children, morals for children, grammars for children, and reading books for children in all languages without number, poetry for children, sermons for children, letters for children, talks for children, and unlimited variations on the same theme, so that the literary doll-shops are crammed all the year round with them, but especially at the time when loving parents and aunts and uncles may be attracted by the appositeness of the notice 'Christmas Gifts for good children.' "

If this is a true picture, it still leaves us craving more information than we have. Not only have most of the early books vanished, but in seeking information about their early illustrations and illustrators, we find that artists of consequence were not interested or used for children's books, nor did the publishers bother to identify the artists on their title pages. Much is known about the adult illustrated books of the eighteenth century; however, we have very few facts about the illustrators of children's books, even though this was one of the rich periods of the illustrated book.

During the middle and latter years of the eighteenth century, book illustration in France enjoyed one of its ages of splendor. Its magnificent productions were created for the noble and rich. Despite the fact that it was an age in which fairy tales were greatly admired, they were thought of as being more suitable for the delectation of the cultured and sophisticated adults than for the young. It was a period of beautiful and costly books. Probably never before or since were so many artists of high talent working on books — engravers like Le Mire, Delauny, and de Longueil; and draughtsman like Oudry, Boucher, Cochin, Moreau, Eisen, Choffard, Gravelot, Le Prince, Monnet, Marillier, and, the greatest of them all, Fragonard. None of these, as far as it is known, published illustrations for children. Children's pictures were still being turned out by routine artists who almost always were anonymous. The brink of the century, however, was to see the entry of the superior artist into the field and the recognition of the importance of his identity.

In England appeared a unique and solitary genius, William Blake (1757-1827), and an artist who was also a technical innovator, Thomas Bewick (1753-1828). In Blake, a towering talent addressed its literary and graphic gifts to the child for the first time, and in Bewick a quiet but positive artistic personality evolved a fresh technique that was to become a commanding means of graphic expression for a hundred years and more. Both these men bridged the eighteenth and nineteenth centuries and were portents of things to come.

Blake defies comparison. His fame has mounted through the years,

WILLIAM BLAKE
*Relief etchings from the Songs of Innocence
and Experience*

but we forget that he speaks to us quite differently from the way he spoke
to his contemporaries. When he printed and colored his extraordinary
little children's books, he had to be content with a scanty audience; his true
audiences were in the future.

Blake printed his *Songs of Innocence* in 1789 and *Songs of
Experience* in 1794 and, driven by the necessity of poverty, worked
out a fresh method of reproduction, the so-called *relief-etching,* which
is somewhat akin to the modern line-cut, without the intervention of
photography. Today it is being revived again by some of our modern
printmakers. In this method, a design is brushed or drawn with a quill

on a metal plate using an acid-resisting varnish as a medium. After the back and edges of the plate are given a protective coat, the metal is immersed in acid and the background is eaten away where not protected by the lines of the design. The action of the acid leaves the design in relief (higher than the background) and when inked will render a printed facsimile. It is difficult to know what the children of Blake's day thought of the *Songs,* or of his pictures for Mary Wollstonecraft's *Original Stories from Real Life.* Their sale was meagre. They speak richly to our age, and modern teachers and librarians have seen to it that Blake's verses and pictures are brought to the attention of today's children.

28

WILLIAM BLAKE
Songs of Innocence and Experience

Thomas Bewick's talent was not a soaring one. He was one of a long line that had celebrated the comfortable beauty of the English countryside. As an apprentice engraver, dissatisfied with the woodcut method of gouging out the white spaces of a design and leaving the lines to be printed in relief, he perfected the *white-line*, a method of using a graver or burin on the end grain of a block to achieve a delicacy of line and a greater range of tone. A combination of a new, attractive technique with the loving delight implicit in his delineation of human, animal, and natural forms won him an enthusiastic audience; and he was busy throughout a long lifetime. A book of his for children was *Pretty Book of Pictures for Little Masters and Misses, or Tommy Trip's*

THOMAS BEWICK
White Line Wood Engravings

29

History of Beasts and Birds. Much of his life's work was devoted to children and he seems to have been the first British artist to be singled out and applauded as an illustrator of children's books. He trained a company of apprentices in his *white-line* engraving technique and they in their turn trained others. From this small source grew the renowned body of skilled wood engravers who by the middle of the nineteenth century were accounting for the bulk of Britain's reproduced pictures and whose illustrations were being imitated both in Europe and America.

THOMAS BEWICK

GEORGE CRUIKSHANK
Modern Illustration
George Bell and Sons

CHAPTER

England After 1800

THE FINE BRITISH GRAPHIC TRADITION was already at full strength with Hogarth, Rowlandson and Blake, but, with the exception of Blake and Bewick, the tradition brought little to the world of children until the beginning of the nineteenth century. Then, a great illustrator appeared and the English audiences of children and grown-ups alike were ready for him.

George Cruikshank (1792-1878) was a remarkable artist born at the right time. As a boy of thirteen he made a sketch of Lord Nelson's funeral; his last drawing was a frontispiece for *The Rose and the Lily,* done in 1875 when he was eighty-three years old. His life spanned a long era of change and expansion, and through it all he drew. George's father Isaac was a caricaturist and etcher who taught George and his brother Robert their trades, but George had a spark of genius denied his father and brother.

His work seemed to delight all ages. Although his children's pictures had none of the prissiness of so many of his contemporaries and more than a touch of the grotesque and macabre, they found large audiences. He fell into his stride when he illustrated the first English editions of the *Märchen* of the Brothers Grimm. From there he went on to *Robinson Crusoe, Cinderella, Puss in Boots,* and a whole gamut of children's writings.

Cruikshank had a rival who pushed him hard enough to annoy

31

him. John Leech (1817-1864) was an indifferent draughtsman but there was a spark in everything he drew. He had a boundless sense of the comic, and there was bounce in even his poorest drawings. He was a regular contributor to *Punch,* but he found time for many other things, including illustrations for *Ingoldsby Legends, Jack the Giant Killer, Cricket on the Hearth* and *Christmas Carol.*

32

JOHN LEECH
Pictures of Life and Character
Bradbury, Agnew and Company

A third rollicking humorist of that time was Richard Doyle (1824-1883) who, like Leech, was a *Punch* contributor and an illustrator of children's books. His work had none of the bite of Cruikshank's, but it was winning and disarming and it can still delight twentieth century eyes.

While Cruikshank, Leech, and Doyle were establishing themselves as sought-after illustrators, the medium of *white-line* engraving on wood, which Bewick had so beautifully perfected, was becoming the major medium of reproduction. Bewick had not only trained a fine group of student engravers, but his work had aroused much admiration and imitation. English engravers were becoming very skillful. Their work was having its influence in Western Europe and the United States. Bewick's own books were exported to other countries, and his blocks were often copied or adapted.

By the middle of the nineteenth century, British books and periodicals were multiplying rapidly. A whole school of younger artists—usually lumped together as the "Illustrators of the Sixties," because much of their best work was done in that decade—appeared to meet the demand. They were a group of great talent. Despite their diverse interests and abilities, there was a common denominator that impressed a superficial similarity on their work and caused them to be thought of as a coherent *school*. This common denominator was the wood-engraving process, which by this time was out of the artist's hands and completely in the control of excellently trained professionals. The professionals were expert but their techniques tended to impose a certain uniformity upon whatever pictorial material they engraved.

The men of the sixties were by no means a closely-knit band such as the Pre-Raphaelites (although there were some Pre-Raphaelites among them). Some, like Charles Keene, Arthur Hughes, and Arthur Boyd Houghton, devoted all, or almost all of their energies to illustration. Others, like Dante Gabriel Rossetti, J. E. Millais, James McNeill Whistler, and Lord Leighton used illustration as a steppingstone to painting. Some were stalwart and forceful draughtsmen like Frederick Sandys and Houghton. Others were sensitive and charming, like George Pinwell and Paul Gray. Some found their material in polite society like George Du Maurier. Others preferred the life of the people like Charles Keene. Almost all these men were strong draughtsmen, and many had a noble sense of composition. The best work of men like Frederick Sandys, Fred Walker, Arthur Boyd Houghton, and Frederick Leighton had superb structure and a sense of inevitable design.

A great deal of the work of these men appeared in the numerous periodicals for both adults and children that were springing up over night — and sometimes vanishing as quickly. Not all these artists drew directly for children but their work appeared largely in so-called *family periodicals*. We have ample evidence that Victorian children fed on this pictorial fare. Moreover, the work done directly for children differed little from that offered to adults. These picturemakers apparently felt little need to adopt a different style for youthful eyes. Arthur Hughes (1832-1915) is remembered mostly for his pictures for George MacDonald's books, notably *At the Back of the North Wind* and *Princess and the Goblin*. He was industrious, consistent, and illustrated many children's texts. At eighty, he was making pictures for the books of George MacDonald's son.

Some of the first commissions of Charles Keene (1823-1891) for children's books came before he had matured, but his later *Don Quixote* contains some of his best work. John Gilbert (1817-1897) illustrated pictures for *Boy's Book of Ballads, Lamb's Tales from Shakespeare, Rhymes for the Nursery*, and numerous fairy tales. Harrison Weir (1824-1906) illustrated many animal books, and Thomas Morten (1836-1866) did a successful *Gulliver's Travels*.

ERNEST GRISET
National Nursery Rhymes
Novello, Ewer

RICHARD DOYLE
Decorative Initial
Richard Doyle
Pellegrini and Cudahy

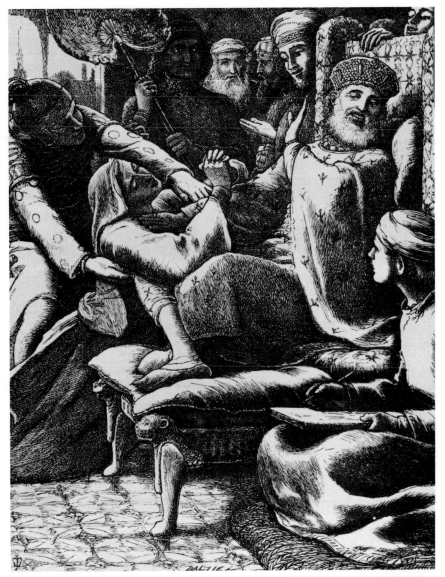

ARTHUR BOYD HOUGHTON
Dalziel's Arabian Nights
Ward, Lock

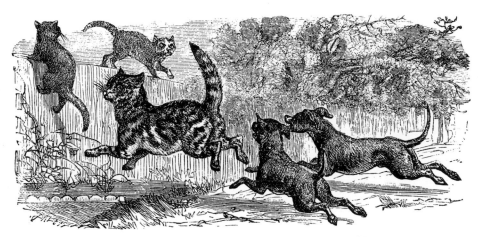

J. B. ZWECKER
National Nursery Rhymes
Novello, Ewer

35

Illustrators' names were now appearing on the title pages of books; publishers, enlightened by the success of Bewick and Cruikshank, realized that many artists now had publics of their own. Characteristic publications of the time were the large, ambitious volumes built around popular texts and crammed with pictures. Some of these books are now handsome monuments of Mid-Victorian days; books like *Dalziel's Arabian Nights* contained a great number of Arthur Boyd Houghton's finest work, and also pictures by Millais, Watson, Tenniel, Pinwell, and Morten. These thick and ponderous volumes were not children's books in the ordinary sense; they were family albums, often placed conspicuously on parlor tables. But good children might be allowed to read them or examine their pictures from time to time. Other books, such as the *National Nursery Rhymes and Nursery Songs,* which had pictures for every song by a long galaxy of artists of the sixties, were not primarily showpieces and could be entrusted to children's hands. From the standpoint of ideal design, these collections of pictures from many sources were scarcely praiseworthy, but leafing through several of them can acquaint one with the illustrative wealth of the sixties.

There is a seriousness and sometimes a ponderous quality about a good deal of Mid-Victorian children's illustration. It would be a great mistake, however, to assume as some have, that all were stuffy and aloof. The best of the more serious illustrations had nobility, drama, and warmth; and side by side with these ran a sparkling current of humor and nonsense. No sooner does one pin a tag on a Victorian characteristic than one is likely to be confronted with its opposite.

Victorian humor had many practitioners but two had a touch of genius: Edward Lear (1812-1888) and Lewis Carroll (Charles Lutwidge Dodgson) (1832-1898). Both Lear and Carroll were excellent examples of the fascinating ambivalence of so many Victorians. Lear, a serious landscape and animal delineator of considerable accomplishment, had a carefree doodling side that was an escape for his delightfully bubbling humor. His use of the limerick form was as irresistible as his drawings, and their combination in his first work, *Book of Nonsense,* brought him popularity and fame.

Lewis Carroll was even a more contrasting personality, on the surface at least. As Charles Lutwidge Dodgson, he was tutor of mathematics at Christ College, Oxford, and author of numerous theoretical treatises. As the writer of *Alice's Adventure in Wonderland* and

EDWARD LEAR
Nonsense Songs, Stories,
Botany and Alphabets
James Osgood and Company

Through the Looking Glass, he reached an enormous audience of children and the child-hearted by playing on the fantasies and absurdities imbedded in unbridled logic.

JOHN TENNIEL
Alice's Adventures in Wonderland
Macmillan

EDWARD LEAR
Nonsense Songs, Stories,
Botany and Alphabets
James Osgood and Company

37

As Percy Muir points out in his *English Children's Books:* "The difference between Dodgson and Carroll is less real than it has been made out to be. In his theoretical treatises, all produced at his own expense and at a loss, his propositions were essentially Carrollian in style, and the elucidations of his problems are humorously worded and interlarded with puns. Indeed it is possible to regard much of his mathematical and logical writing as a series of trial runs for the gloriously logical absurdities which are the foundation of the Alice stories. In them, we see him fully aware of the ridiculous situations produced by taking words in their literal meanings, by regarding them, as he was apt to do in his serious writings, as symbols or counters in a mathematical problem."

Like Lear, Carroll could draw, but not as successfully. He did make pictures for his books, but aware of his limitations, looked for a better artist and found the ideal one. John Tenniel (1820-1914) was a good workmanlike illustrator, above average but scarcely inspired. He contributed pictures to a number of books and for years his rather stately political cartoons were a full-page feature of *Punch.* Carroll's texts proved to be an ideal vehicle for his talent. They brought out his best and resulted in a definitive collaboration. Tenniel's Alice pictures have none of the usual artifices of humorous drawings. Faithfully presenting the situations of Carroll's text in a straightforward technique, they have about them a disarming enchantment that few have been able to resist. Carroll's and Tenniel's Alice is a monument to the neglected side of Victorianism, the deep well of laughter behind the portentous facade.

As the sixties faded into the seventies, the school of the sixties, although it did not cease, made less impact as a group and most of its artists became less concerned with the children's world. That world soon came to be dominated by a trio of artists: Walter Crane (1845-1915), Randolph Caldecott (1846-1886), and Kate Greenaway (1846-1901). With them the power and sense of the structure of the sixties disappeared and a pictorial world of charm, cheerfulness, and bland, scrubbed faces took its place. The men of the sixties loved the quirks of human character and the infinitely varied movements of the human frame; the new trio made do with a few stereotyped characters and a predictable repertoire of poses. The world they created was cozy and appealing, without stress, strain, or question.

It was their and our good fortune that these three artists had almost all their best work reproduced by Edmund Evans, engraver and color-printer. Evans' great improvements on the earlier woodblock color printing processes of Baxter and other earlier pioneers produced a revolution in color printing. Under Evans' coaching, the three artists learned to prepare their originals in a way that would permit the new process to show its best effects, and the result was a long series of unusually charming children's books. The colors were soft and attractive, the textures pleasant; and the somewhat overcrowded Victorian sense of page design disarmed rigid criticism.

It is no wonder that these books were popular and that the reputations of these three artists grew. Walter Crane found his subject matter in fairy tales, legends, and similar material. He had a sober imagination which never reached a point of excitement. Fond of elaboration, he had a particular appetite for involved borders. He was not only a prolific illustrator but found time for teaching, lecturing, and writing numerous children's books and several volumes on his profession, illustration.

WALTER CRANE
The First of May
James Osgood and Company

Randolph Caldecott and Kate Greenaway found their subject matter in an English world of a nostalgic and imagined past. Theirs was a prettified version of the English countryside, with its traditional neatness and picturesqueness, inhabited by cheerful and uncomplicated grownups and clean starchy children. Caldecott had a wider repertoire of faces, situations, and backgrounds than Kate Greenaway, for her world was a very pruned and selected one. Her reputation became much greater than Crane's and Caldecott's and still is. Her work was greatly admired by Ruskin, although he was not blind to her deficiencies and he wrote her about them in numerous letters. He told her, "Nobody wants anatomy, but you can't get on without form." "You ought to make notes of groups of children—you should go to some watering place in August with fine sands and draw no end of bare feet." He asked for "flowers that won't look as if their leaves had been in curl papers all night," for "shoes that weren't quite so like mussel shells," for "girls that should be drawn with limbs as well as frocks."

These three artists set a pattern for the children's picture books of their time and they had many imitators. They were minor artists but delightful ones, and they probably ripened to the limit of their restricted abilities in the warmth of a wide and receptive audience.

RANDOLPH CALDECOTT
Drawing in collection of the author

For the young people who had outgrown Greenaway, Caldecott, and Crane, there were quite a number of other able figure illustrators such as Gordon Browne (1858-1932), Charles (1870-1938) and Henry Brock (1875-), Henry M. Paget (1857-1936), and Hugh Thomson (1860-1920). Thomson, the most highly regarded of them, illustrated a long line of classics with taste and authority. He illustrated a *Jack the Giant Killer* and *Tom Brown's School Days,* but many of his adult books were the kind that would be read by precocious older children. The Brocks' technique and pictorial outlook was very similar to Thomson's, while Browne and Paget, more vigorous and concerned with movement, gravitated toward a dramatic and adventurous kind of text.

A new note was struck in illustration when William Nicholson (1872-) used his knowledge of poster design to make a group of picture books in flat, subdued colors, bounded by fat black lines. The ordinary editions of his books were printed by lithographers, but there were smaller editions printed from wood blocks in line and colored by hand. They are illustrative high lights of the end of the century.

With the opening of the new century and the rapid improvement in the photoengraving processes, a new type of picture book replaced

HUGH THOMSON
Pride and Prejudice

41

WILLIAM NICHOLSON
An Alphabet
Heinemann

the charming wood block printings of Evans. Although this was in some ways an aesthetic loss, the new four, or full-color process was naturally taken advantage of by a newer breed of artists. Three of unusual abilities began their rapid climbs to fame: Beatrix Potter (1866-1943), Arthur Rackham (1867-1939), and finally Edmund Dulac (1882-1953).

Quietly but persuasively, Beatrix Potter's pictures and little tales have won their way into the hearts of countless thousands of children. In her modest way she held the key to the door of a diminutive world of magic kinship with the little things of the earth, of the loving mystery of growing and moving life. Janet Adam Smith, in *Children's Illustrated Books,* says, "Beatrix Potter did more than mirror a region in her pictures; she supplied the *genius loci* in her enchanting animals. Is it absurdly fanciful to think of them as the English equivalents of fawns and nymphs whose legends express the sentiment of a scene or landscape?.... She has in full measure Samuel Palmer's gift of suffusing a landscape with innocence and happiness."

Beatrix Potter, and in his way, too, Arthur Rackham seem to have drawn deeply from that subterranean current of the earth's poetry that runs through the depths of the English subconsciousness. It has risen to the surface in so much of their poetry and prose, less often in their art. It is an ancient stream but perpetually fresh.

Rackham is less specific about the concrete world than Beatrix Potter and more contrived, but his never-never world has more substance and conviction than those of Randolph Caldecott or Kate Greenaway. We can walk into it and believe in it as we can in Lewis Carroll's world. It may not be the world of every day life, but it is convincing.

Beatrix Potter's books were appropriately tiny and unpretentious. Rackham's and Dulac's were large, handsome volumes which proclaimed their expensiveness. The successors to the Victorian gift albums, they became something of a badge of culture. Their books were well designed, well printed and more worthy examples of the illustrator's and designer's art than most critics of today may admit.

There was a world of difference between the styles of Potter and Rackham and that of Edmund Dulac. French by birth, Dulac was a consummate decorator. He had an eclectic thirst for the art of the past, and incorporated his knowledge into a remarkable vocabulary of design

BEATRIX POTTER
Two Bad Mice
F. Warne and Company

ARTHUR RACKHAM
Peer Gynt
J. P. Lippincott

forms. His work had a cosmopolitan air, new in English illustration, but it found a large audience. Although he indulged his sumptuous color sense in book after book of full-color process plates, his less frequent line drawings showed him to be a sensitive draughtsman as well.

The popularity of the large, expensive gift book waned as color in children's books became more common. Gradually the offset methods began to usurp the place that letterpress and process engraving had previously held in the picture-book field. Relatively inexpensive picture

EDMUND DULAC
The Real Princess
Hodder and Stoughton

books of comparatively few pages became common. Today there are many artists in this field. Their standard of performance is high, but can we find any giants?

For a while some considered Claud Lovat Fraser (1890-1921) a giant, for his *Nursery Rhymes* and *Peacock Pie* with their pictures in bold outlines enclosing bright, flat color areas in the manner of the old chapbooks, caused a furor in the twenties. They seemed very novel, as something reminiscent of the past often does, and it is true that they were very lively and captivating books. But Fraser was a stringently limited artist, who was not able to develop in his short span of life the potentialities he may have possessed. His American imitator, Elizabeth MacKinstry, had a brief fame in the children's book world. William Russell Flint (1880-) was in high favor with a segment of the book public, but he was hardly a children's artist and once past the virtuosity of his water color little remains. Eric Ravilious might have gone far, but his early death ended his brief career as an illustrator.

For about two generations England boasted a remarkable school of wood engraving, studded with fine talents, but this brilliant renaissance of wood engraving did little for the children's book. Only Joan Hassall (1906-) and Gwen Raverat (1885-1957) seem to have devoted much time to children's problems. Agnes Miller-Parker illustrated *The Fables of Aesop* for the Gregynog Press and David Jones engraved blocks for *Gulliver's Travels* for the Golden Cockerel Press. Most of

JOAN HASSALL
Our Village
George G. Harrap and Company

GWEN RAVERAT
Bird Talisman
Faber and Faber

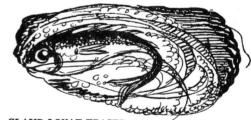

CLAUD LOVAT FRASER
Poems
Poetry Bookshop

45

this large and gifted group produced their designs for the special and limited edition presses and so remained outside the children's book world.

The illustrators and designers for the private presses and limited editions have the better of it; they have more freedom, better materials to work with, and the critics notice them. Still we tend to forget that it is the trade-book illustrators who bear the heat and brunt of the day. They work, usually, with insufficient time, second rate materials, and little appreciation. When they surmount their handicaps they deserve double praise. English illustration has had a hard core of artists who have had the high competence to accept the difficulties of commercial publishing without losing the power to make a personal statement: graphic men like Ernest Shepard, Edward Bawden, Eric Fraser, Robin Jacques, Mervyn Peake, Rowland Hilder, S. Walter Hodges, and Edward Ardizzone.

Ernest Shepard (1879-) was born when the Caldecott influence was in its ascendancy. He must have grown up surrounded by it, for he continued the tradition with brilliance as a mature artist. He became famous with his illustrations for the Kenneth Grahame and A. A. Milne books. They have unflagging sprightliness and humor. He drew thousands of illustrations, and seems never to have had a bad day.

Edward Bawden (1903-), a talented illustrator, has a method, but keeps fresh. He has used his design abilities in many fields, and he knows what to do with a book. His humor, usually just a twinkle, often means more than the insistent kind.

ERNEST H. SHEPARD
The Wind in the Willows
Charles Scribner's Sons

46

EDWARD BAWDEN

Another illustrator with a strong design sense is Eric Fraser (1902-). His richly involved illustrations have a handsome medieval modernism which accords with his usually romantic subject matter.

The work of Robin Jacques (1920-) and Mervyn Peake (1911-) has a certain similarity. Both artists have a careful and rounded pen technique, and a certain grotesque humor lurks behind their meticulous drawings.

C. Walter Hodges (1909-) and Rowland Hilder (1905-) are strong draughtsmen and vigorous technicians, whose sturdiness and sense of movement appeal to older boys. Mr. Hodges is as capable an author as he is an artist.

In the English tradition, too, are the delightful pen drawings of Edward Ardizzone (1900-). A prolific and ebullient artist, he has also supplied his own texts for a long series of children's books. Some of his work has been in color, reproduced by lithography, but his work is essentially in black and white with color applied over a monochrome framework.

One of the heirs of the great English tradition of graphic draughtsmenship and a brilliant exponent of it is Ronald Searle (1920-). A caricaturist of great power, his range of subject matter is wide. He is considered strong medicine by some adults, who would probably object to listing such books as the St. Trinian's series and *Down With Skool* as fare for children. They are about children as monsters, and the young are known to rejoice in these portraits of themselves. Another humorous graphic artist of wide appeal is Rowland Emett (1906-) whose droll pictures of antiquated trains have delighted children and grownups alike.

The Penguin books have made publishing history not only in the adult world but also in the children's. Their Puffin books, while not uniformly successful, have maintained a generally high standard and have occasionally been triumphs of inexpensive bookmaking. In this long series are such excellent examples as *The Arabs*, with designs by

RONALD SEARLE
The Terror of St. Trinians
Max Parrish

Edward Bawden; *Trees in Britain*, written and drawn by S. R. Badmin; *A Child's Alphabet*, designed by Grace Gabler; *Zoo Animals*, with very beautiful drawings by Maurice Wilson; *Heads, Bodies & Legs*, by Denis Wirth-Miller and Richard Chopping; and *Extinct Animals*, written and illustrated by Hilary Stebbing.

David Bland, in his *History of Book Illustration*, says, "The most original illustration of today both in Britain and America, however, is in the big books for the very young, which rely on pictures rather than text. Here long runs make it possible to print several colors, generally by lithography, in a style that seems to have come to the West from Russia. Significantly it was two Polish artists, Lewitt and Him, who provided the pictures for one of the most popular books in this class, Diana Ross's *The Little Red Engine gets a Name* (1942)."

There has been a long succession of excellent books of this variety: Hilary Stebbing's *Monty's New House*; Alan Howard's *The Story of Peter and the Wolf*; Priscilla Thornycroft's *Whiskers the Cat*; *Old Winkle and the Seagulls*, by the Roses; V. H. Drummond's *Little Laura on the River*; and *Orlando the Marmalade Cat: A Trip Abroad*, written and illustrated by Kathleen Hale, are only a few.

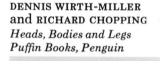

DENNIS WIRTH-MILLER
and RICHARD CHOPPING
Heads, Bodies and Legs
Puffin Books, Penguin

LEWITT-HIM
The Little Red Engine Gets a Name
Faber and Faber

MAURICE WILSON
Zoo Animals
Puffin Books, Penguin

GRACE GABLER
A Child's Alphabet
Puffin Books, Penguin

49

Both in Britain and in America there has been an increasing stream of these books as the child audience has grown. Spread around a large exhibition hall these titles would make a brave and colorful show, irresistible to the eyes of child and parent. But they come and go like the season's leaves, bright and captivating for the moment but tending to be forgotten. Their texts are usually of little consequence; it is their illustrations we are struck by. The pictures of these new books are intended for instant appeal and successfully so. More and more often, however, they seem to be the results of a conscious naivete that is beginning to pall. The legitimate craving for freshness a few decades ago has brought about a determined and contrived pursuit of freshness, which is beginning to defeat its purpose. One gets the feeling that a brilliant age of children's books is becoming the victim of its success and that a new one is forming behind the polychrome of the present facade.

PRISCILLA THORNYCROFT
Whiskers the Cat
Burk

LUDWIG RICHTER
Deutsche Art und Sitte
Verlag von Alphons Dürr

CHAPTER 4

Europe From 1800 On

THE EARLY YEARS OF THE NINETEENTH CENTURY saw rapid changes, for the French Revolution had shaken much of Europe's political structure and the rapidly rising tide of romanticism was fracturing old concepts and refashioning art, music, and literature. The relatively homogeneous eighteenth century passed into a time of multiple trends and diversified expressions.

Children were getting more books and, gradually, better ones. For centuries Europe's children had been peering into the world of faëry, opened to them by the tales told by their parents or nurses, but little of this lore found its way into their more substantial books. Only the cheap chapbooks bothered to recount the old tales. Curiously enough, during the eighteenth century sumptuously illustrated editions of fairy tales were available to grown-ups, particularly in France, where La Fontaine's fables and Perrault's tales were fashionable in cultivated circles.

With the new century, interest in old tales and legends increased. First the Brothers Grimm, Jakob (1785-1863), Wilhelm (1786-1859), collected their *Marchen*, and then Hans Christian Andersen (1805-1875) published his tales. Earlier, the *Thousand and One Nights* had been translated into French. Now a simplified and expurgated version of it was made available for children. But the fairy tale, whether of Perrault the Frenchman, Andersen the Dane, or the German Grimm

51

Brothers, could not be kept within national borders. It would be translated and retranslated and soon become the property of all European children.

Germany, in particular, gave full rein to the fairy tale for children. Her publishers and artists took advantage of Senefelder's discovery of the new reproductive process of lithography, and German chromolithography for children's books set a fashion that spread through western Europe. Theodor Hosemann used hand-lithography successfully for his children's books, as did Ebeling for *Gesammette Schriften* in 1857; but the most popular of the lithographed books of the nineteenth century was Heinrich Hoffman-Donner's *Struwwelpeter*. Hoffman (1809-1894) was by profession neither a writer nor an artist, but a physician who drew pictures and told stories to soothe his small patients. He was astute enough, when his sketches were published, to insist that the lithographer copy them exactly "to ensure that my amateurish style is not artistically improved and idealized." *Struwwelpeter* is still in print in many of the world's languages.

DR. HEINRICH HOFFMANN
Struwwelpeter
Im Infel

52

WILHELM BUSCH
Balduin Bahlamm

LUDWIG RICHTER
Fürs Haus

The illustrative giant of Germany in the nineteenth century was Adolf Von Menzel (1815-1905), but he seems to have ignored the children's field. Another German artist, a sentimentally charming children's book illustrator, was Ludwig Richter (1803-1884). His blond cherubs and picturesque backgrounds in clean line delighted children and adults of his time and his works are still collector's items. A children's artist of radically different gifts was Wilhelm Busch (1832-1908), a rollicking, rambunctious humorist. His slapstick and galloping drawing has been compared to Edward Lear's, but the comparison is scarcely apt. Busch is more earthy and less subtle. He drew many of his pictures in strip series, a trick he learned from the Swiss, Rodolphe Topffer (1799-1846). Topffer was not only an engaging picturemaker for children, but he was supposed to be the originator of the comic strip. If this is true, his influence has undoubtedly spread beyond his wildest imaginings.

In Denmark, the only important illustrators were Kay Nielsen (1886-), with his stylized colored pictures for old fairy tales, and Hans Tegner (1853-1932), who produced illustrations worthy of the text of Hans Christian Andersen's tales. It is interesting to note the fate of children's texts in their search for definitive illustration. Hans Andersen's first illustrator was mediocre, and many other artists tried their hands at his tales, all with little success. The tales waited until 1900 for Tegner's pictures. *Pinocchio's* first illustrations were unremarkable. The best perhaps were E. Mazzanti's, but the story still awaits its definite hand. Few books got off to the perfect start of *Alice in Wonderland*, although the Grimm Brothers' first English edition luckily fell into the hands of Cruikshank. George MacDonald's *At the Back of the North Wind* was perfect for Arthur Hughes, and no one has bettered Howard Pyle's *Robin Hood*. But *Robinson Crusoe* and *Gulliver's Travels* are still being competed for, despite the many artists who have done quite well by them.

HANS TEGNER

KAY NIELSEN
East of the Sun and West of the Moon
Doran

France, throughout the nineteenth century, was an active center of book illustrations. Few of its better artists, however, devoted their talents to the children's book. Exceptions were the pictures of J. I. Grandville (1803-1847) for *Robinson Crusoe* and *Gulliver's Travels*, Pauquet's charming animal vignettes, and the *Don Quixote* of Tony Johannot (1803-1852). Undoubtedly, a caricaturist and humorist like Caran d'Ache delighted children on the sly, and we may include him when he gives us such a disarming title as *Album Pour les Enfants de Quarante Ans et Au-dessus.*

But the idolized illustrator of the latter half of the century was Paul Gustave Doré (1833-1883). No illustrator up to his time had such widespread influence; his books were sold in great numbers in England, America, and throughout Europe. With a few exceptions his volumes were large-paged, bulky, and generously pictured. His fairy tale subjects were produced for adults as well as children. They were meant for the parlor table and polite family consumption. But we

GUSTAVE DORE
*Original illustration
from the collection
of the author*

know from countless sources that the children took over Doré, and several generations of them were enchanted by his pictures.

Doré, once the most applauded illustrator of his day, is now treated with indifference. His faults have been exaggerated, his virtues minimized; but he had magnificent gifts that cannot be ignored. No illustrator today could hope to match his incredible fecundity and wide-ranging draughtsmanship.

The twentieth century in France has been a flourishing and fruitful period for the illustrated limited-editions book. The finest materials and press work have been lavished on these books and they show the work of many distinguished illustrators and painters at their best. The trade editions and children's books suffer by comparison, but even in these fields there still has been a body of important work. In the early years of the century, the delicate outlines and flat colors of the work of Boutet de Monvel (1850-1913) were notable, as in his *Jeanne d'Arc* and *Nos Enfants*. Later, Carlegle illustrated some books for children, and the painter Paul Bonnard did at least two. Job [Jacques Onfray de Bréville (1858-1931)] had a sumptuous pictorial sense. His long series of historical picture books have revealed the country's past to several generations of French children. Pierre Brissaud (1885-), the Belgian, Jean de Bosschère (1878-), Maurice Leloir (1853-1940), Albert Robida (1848-1926), and Guy Arnoux have all made important contributions to trade editions and children's books.

A great romantic illustrator, Edy Legrand (1893-), has done many books for children. His *Voyages et Glorieuses Découvertes Des Grand Navigateurs et Explorateurs Français* was a landmark which influenced illustration far beyond the borders of France. Other interesting books of his are *Macao et Cosmage, L'Ile Rose, Lafayette,* and *La Nuit de la St. Sylvain.* The fine Père Castor series with color-lithographs by Feodor Rojankovsky (1891-) struck a new note and were widely imitated, but when the artist Rojankovsky and the editor, Georges Duplaix moved to the United States, that type of book design found a new home. André François (1915-) and Etienne Morel are among the best of contemporary children's book illustrators. The death of Jean de Brunhoff (1899-1937), the creator of the Babar Series, removed an artist and writer whose fame has spread throughout the world.

56

JEAN DE BRUNHOFF
Babar books
Random House

M. BOUTET DE MONVEL
Jeanne D'Arc
Plon-Nourrit & Cie

EDY LEGRAND
Little Story of Lafayette
Tolmer

In the earlier years of the century, Germany and Austria produced some noteworthy children's books by artists such as Max Slevogt, Christian Morgenstern, Elsa Eisgruber, Ernst Kreidolf, and Walter Trier; but two wars and Hitler's purge decimated the ranks of the illustrators severely. No country could lose such artists as H. Steiner-Prag, Fritz Kredel, Hans Mueller, William Sharp, Fritz Eichenberg, Kurt Wiese, Richard Floethe, Jan Balet, and others who migrated to the United States, without impoverishing its creative powers.

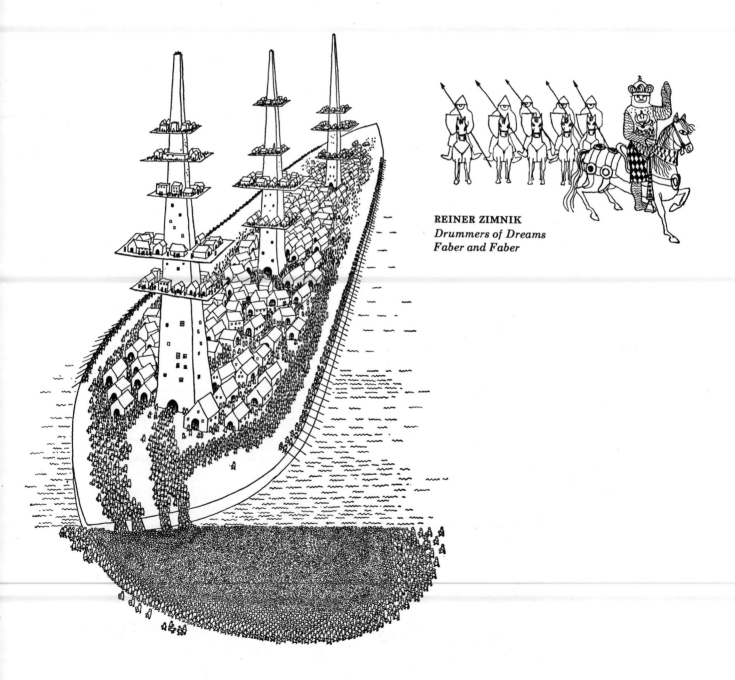

REINER ZIMNIK
Drummers of Dreams
Faber and Faber

Recently, Germany's children's publications have grown. We encounter personalities like Reiner Zimnik (1930-) whose rollicking, effortless lines have animated such books as *Xaver der Ringelstecher und das gelbe Ross, Jonas der Angler,* and *Drummers of Dreams.* Some of Zimnik's books have been reprinted in England and the United States. The imaginative drawings of Gerhard Oberlaender, particularly in his *Pienchen* and *Pingo und Pongo,* are popular with German children. Fritz Busse has charmingly illustrated a child's book and other artists with special gifts are the East German, Joseph Hegenbarth, a compelling and persuasive draughtsman; Eugen Sporer and Wiltrand Jasper, talented woodcutters; and Werner Labbe, with his playful outlines.

The Scandinavian countries had some artists of high caliber. The Norwegian Louis Moe (1857-1945), the Swedish Carl Larsson (1853-1919) and John Bauer (1882-1918). Louis Moe's drawings are irresistible in their charm and humor. The scampering animals and children communicate their relish for life and delight in muscular joy. Larsson is placid and sedate by comparison, but wins us with his love of homely things and warm contented people. Bauer never received the widespread attention his work deserved. His illustrations of the haunted northern forests inhabited by doltish trolls are as captivating and convincing as any portrait of fairyland that could be named. Of today's Scandinavian illustrators, Denmark's Arne Ungermann (1902-) seems one of the greatest. His justly praised and popular *Kavanki-vanki* ranks him with the greatest. Sikken Hansen, Mogens Zieler, and Erik Blegvad are three more Danish artists whose work deserves mention, together with the Swedish Bertil Almquist.

JOHN BAUER
Bästa
Ahlén & Akerlunds Förlag

There is probably rich material in Poland, Russia, and Czechoslovakia. Enough has emerged from these countries to have had an influence on western European and American illustration, but our information is fragmentary. Illustrators like the Czech Jire Trnka, whose work in *Kormidelnik Vlnosky* and *Rikejte si Pohadky,* kindles our interest, and the Poles, Olga Siemaszko, Eryk Lipinski, and Adam Kilian make us wish to know more about children's books in those countries. Russia, whose children's books aroused Western enthusiasm two generations ago, seems to have lost the touch of freshness and inspiration in their illustrative material. A recent Soviet Exposition in New York exhibited several hundred books, but there was almost nothing to excite our interest.

All over Europe, as in America, a greater volume of children's books is being printed than ever before. There is a plentiful supply of illustrative talent—it becomes difficult not only to see the forest because of the trees, but to see all the trees. National characteristics tend to soften and melt into a cosmopolitan conformity. There is considerable exchange of books and publication rights between countries; and, except for the Iron Curtain countries, it is easier now than ever before to find the work of foreign artists in one's own bookstores and libraries. Although it is stimulating to see so many excellent books appear year after year, there is still a great gulf between the best and the worst.

JIRE TRNKA

Woodcut of Richard Mather
The earliest known
American illustration

CHAPTER 5

America—the Earlier Years

NO ONE EXPECTS MUCH OF THE ARTS in America's earliest years. Indeed, in the light of its wilderness background, it is difficult to imagine the magnitude of effort that must have been expended in order to bring forth even the early crude beginnings of an American art. Scholars, combing through the evidence of the wilderness years, have found what seems to be our first illustration, a humble woodcut done of Richard Mather in 1670, and our first book illustration, a 1677 woodcut map of New England. A few years later, in 1682, we find a book for children, *The Rule of the New Creatures*, printed in Boston by Mary Avery, the first woman publisher in America, and in 1684 John Cotton's *Spiritual Milk for American Babes*, another children's book. The dates are important, because they show us how early the presses were busy in New England, and how soon after the settlement days a concern for children's minds showed itself. The books are without pictures, and reading the old texts is an effort today. We are too far from the seventeenth-century climate to understand easily what appeal these words could have had for those young minds.

As the eighteenth unfolds, the books for children multiply; in fact, they seem to number a sizable proportion of the total output. Pictures (woodcuts) appear, and later some copper engravings. They are quaint to our eyes; little else can be said of them. There seems to have been no American draughtsman or engraver of stature in those

61

years. Many pictures are inept copies of English blocks. In fact, a great many of these early books were copies or adaptations of British books that had been popular.

For instance, Jacob Johnson, a Quaker, was publishing children's books in 1780 which were reprints and revisions of London publications that went as far back as 1688. In 1760, Hugh Gaine of New York was importing many of John Newbery's juvenile books and two years later was reprinting them. We know little about the size of these editions. They must have been small; and yet it has been estimated that perhaps six million copies of one book, the *American New England Primer*, were printed between 1688, when it was first issued, and 1830, when it finally went out of print.

As the century moved past the Revolution and into the years of the young Republic, the books multiplied, but their quality showed small improvement. There was little sign of an authentic hand or an individual touch. Not until the early years of the nineteenth century did we encounter the first authentic personality in American graphic art. Alexander Anderson (1775-1870), a New York physician turned engraver, was captivated by the new style of *white-line* engraving perfected by Thomas Bewick and he copied and reinterpreted many of

ALEXANDER ANDERSON
*Wood engraving by the artist
of himself
in his eighty-fourth year*

*A page from a children's A.B.C.
distributed by a patent medicine firm.
An early advertising gambit, circa 1860*

62

ALEXANDER ANDERSON
Wood engravings from early books

Typical early cheap booklet for children, decorated with hand-colored woodcuts. Paper covers. No date

THE PLOUGHMAN.

The ploughman's labor first prepares
    The bosom of the earth for seed;
This done, he has no farther cares,
    And other laborers succeed.

The well-ploughed furrow shows his skill—
    Which process finishes his toil;
It is his task the ground to till,
    Nor further cultivate the soil.

Bewick's blocks. He struck out on his own, too, with varying success; his talent was by no means of Bewick's calibre, but many of his engravings have considerable charm. He was prolific throughout a long life; and although most of his work was for adults, his books included a *Mother Goose* and a *Children's Friend*. Generally considered America's first engraver of consequence, he may also be called our first professional illustrator.

During the first forty years of the nineteenth century, illustrated children's books increased in number but there was a similarity about them. Many of them were anonymous and gave no credit to the artists. A large proportion—perhaps as high as forty or fifty percent—of the children's books sold in the United States during the 1840's came from England.

63

In the forties, however, the first American illustrator of real attainment appeared on the scene. He was Felix Octavius Darley (1822-1888) whose pictures, engraved on wood by William Croome, appeared in *Peter Ploddy and Other Oddities*, published in Philadelphia in 1844. Darley, a prolific illustrator for a great many years, illustrated works by Cooper, Dickens, Irving, Poe, Longfellow, and other much-read authors, many in large and expensive gift-book editions. He also had his children's audience in books like Dodge's *Hans Brinker*, Edgeworth's *Moral Tales*, and Moore's, *Visit from St. Nicholas*.

By the middle of the nineteenth century, children's illustrators were encouraged by the appearance of a number of children's magazines which offered wider scope for their work. In 1865 appeared *Our Young Folks*, which, eight years later, merged with *St. Nicholas* to become a selective and receptive vehicle for children's stories and pictures until its suspension in 1930. *The Riverside Magazine for Young People* had a brief, but notable career and *Harper's Young People* flourished until the last year of the century. These magazines

WINSLOW HOMER
Our Young Folks. 1867

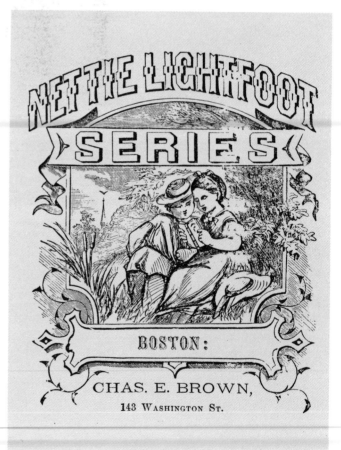

Title page by unknown artist for a typical series of children's books of the middle 19th century

FELIX DARLEY Two preliminary sketches for children's illustrations for *Hop O' My Thumb* (above) and for *The Children's Hour* (right). At top, engraving from a finished drawing for Irving's, "Washington."

65

HOWARD PYLE
Harper's Young People

and such latecomers as *The Youth's Companion* and *John Martin's Book* were valuable outlets and training grounds for young illustrators.

Children's books became livelier after the Civil War, but the major breakthrough in children's illustration had to wait until the late seventies and eighties when photoengraving methods were developed. Older men, like the great cartoonist Thomas Nast (1840-1902), and the indefatigable Felix Darley were doing a lion's share of the work, but a brilliant group of young artists was serving its apprenticeship under Charles Parsons, the art director at Harper and Brothers. Edwin A. Abbey, Howard Pyle, William A. Rogers, George Luks, Charles Stanley Reinhart, Arthur B. Frost, William Smedley, and Edward B. Kemble were a group that knew and were influenced by each other. Presently each would go his own individual way toward the fulfillment of his gifts and contribute his share of lustre to a fine period of illustration; but for the time being, they learned from each other, struck sparks from mutual contact, and sharpened themselves for the life work ahead.

Darley was joined about fifteen years later by another illustrator of first rank, Winslow Homer (1836-1910), whose first book design was a title page for a series of children's books. Darley and Homer were in many ways artistic opposites; Darley was elegant, Homer forthright and simple. Darley drew his strength from European tradition, Homer formed his own ways. But these two fine talents, different in so many ways, enabled us to match some of the European illustrations for the first time.

CHAPTER **6**

Howard Pyle and the Brandywine Tradition

THE INVENTION OF PHOTOENGRAVING in the last quarter of the nineteenth century made it possible for American illustrators to meet the mounting demand for printed pictures by our expanding population. It was the country's good fortune that at the moment there were available a group of artists of high excellence who threw their talents and energies into the new art. In that gifted group was one of giant proportions—Howard Pyle (1853-1911). In the field of children's books he made immensely important contributions both as illustrator and writer, and many of his books are still in circulation. In addition, he taught and inspired a large group of talented artists whose work and teaching has been passed on into the third, fourth, and fifth generations.

Pyle was a Quaker from Wilmington, Delaware, American in bone, sinew and mind. He lived to create a large body of pictures as solid and American as himself. He became a great and prolific picture-maker, whose natural gifts were wedded to an unyielding sense of devotion and an enormous capacity for work—a combination that made him the captain of a growing school of young illustrators. He wrote stories and books, many becoming classics of children's literature. He gathered about him a company of young talent, trained them, and sent them out into the world to spread his pictorial gospel. He became not only the most important force in the illustration of his day, but a continuing force that is still felt in some of our present-day work.

Pyle grew up at a time and in a place that nourished his native feeling for the land, its people, and their handiwork. Wilmington, where he was born in 1853, was only a town, growing toward city size, still retaining much of the flavor of earlier days. Behind the town was the valley of the Brandywine, threading its way inland into Pennsylvania between wooded hills and horse-plowed fields. Conestoga wagons filled with lime still rolled down the roads from Lancaster County. It was easy to feel an earlier America in the old houses, the cobbled streets, and the stone farmhouses and barns of the valley.

Young Pyle breathed in this atmosphere and it filled him to the brim. It filled him with a wonder and love for old worn things; for wind, weather, and sky, for stone walls and shingle roofs, for the feel of handmade things; and, above all, for people. He drew strength, too, from the old legends of Europe; and it was these, passing through his lively mind, that were the core of so many of his books for children. These old tales had been told many times but a Victorian aura of anemic sentiment and routine moralizing enveloped most of them. This damp and chilly atmosphere was swept away by the health and good spirits of Pyle's texts and pictures. There was a clean wind blowing in them, a bright and golden light, and a sturdiness and solidity of form.

His early *Robin Hood* was an instant success with its meaty and heart-warming bounce. It was followed by *Pepper and Salt* and *Wonder Clock,* two delightful collections of Pyle-invented tales crowded with captivating pen drawings; *Otto of the Silver Hand;* the four volumes of the *King Arthur* tales; *Men of Iron; A Modern Alladin;* and *Jack Ballister's Fortunes.* All except the last three were well designed from cover to cover, each an integrated unit of text and picture, each imparting vigorous new life to older traditions of bookmaking.

It is interesting to note that the earlier Pyle books were much finer examples of book design that the later ones. They were hearty and honest in their arrangement of type and pictures, free of false elegance, the work of a strong hand. The pictures in sturdy pen line enhanced with a few simple pen tones and a rich feeling for pattern cooperated well with the simply set text. But the later books were illustrated by halftones tipped into the text, and a sense of unity disappeared from the books. This happened not only with Pyle, but generally in the field, and can be considered a matter of a technological process overpowering other considerations. The halftone had become

Sir Kay breaketh his sword. at ye Tournament.

HOWARD PYLE
King Arthur and his Knights
Charles Scribner's Sons

69

perfected, the publishers were proud of it, the public liked it, and the artists, with a new marvel that reproduced their tonal drawings so well, were beguiled into abandoning the ink line and reveling in tonal wash and oil. It was not the first, nor will it be the last time that a technological improvement has smothered art.

Beyond the wide-spreading authority of Pyle's pictures and texts was the impetus he gave to the education of illustrators. Although there was now an urgent demand for competent illustrators, the means for their training were meager. Pyle began with some classes held at the Drexel Institute in Philadelphia but soon felt the need to work with a select group and have complete responsibility for them. He gathered about him a gifted company of men and women, whom he taught without pay in his studios in Wilmington and Chadd's Ford. Soon these students began to move out into the field, and a pronounced Howard Pyle flavor became apparent in much of American illustration. Some of them imitated the Pyle characteristics, others began by imitation and developed their own individuality; many had fine, independent gifts which Pyle strengthened. He spent little time with technique or style. He drove into the heart and meaning of their pictures, teaching them to breathe life into their conceptions. A favorite phrase of his was, "Throw your heart into your picture and jump in after it."

He kindled a fire in most of these young people that warmed them for the rest of their lives. Some caught no more than the letter of his evangelism, others the spirit, but it was a growing and powerful force for several generations and it still persists.

HOWARD PYLE
Harper's Young People

70

FRANK SCHOONOVER
Robinson Crusoe
Penn Publishing Company

N. C. WYETH
Black Arrow
Charles Scribner's Sons

The names of most of these students are now part of our illustrative history. Among those who went on to contribute to the art of children's books were Jessie Willcox Smith, N. C. Wyeth, Frank E. Schoonover, Stanley Arthurs, Thornton Oakley, Edward Wilson, Maxfield Parrish and Pyle's own sister, Katharine.

Of them all, N. C. Wyeth (1882-1945) made the most important contribution. His long series of children's classics for Scribner's, illustrated with full-color process plates and sometimes with additional chapter headings in pen and ink, were very popular with children and had large sales. Many of the titles are still in print. His *Treasure Island, Kidnapped, White Company, Black Arrow, Drums, Deerslayer,* and *Last of the Mohicans* are well remembered volumes.

Frank Schoonover (1877-) illustrated a series of boys' books which were outwardly similar to Wyeth's Scribner's series. In fact, this had become a standardized format for the *gift book* type. Jessie Willcox Smith (1863-1935) made a reputation with her delineation of immaculate young girls and boys in a similar series of large books, possibly the best of which was Stevenson's *Child's Garden of Verses.* Some of the most interesting and individual of this type were those of Maxfield Parrish (1870-); highly colored pictures for Kenneth Grahame's *Dream Days,* and *Arabian Nights.* Katherine Pyle (1863-1938) was greatly influenced by her brother's bold and decorative pen style in *Wonder Clock* and *Pepper and Salt.* She practiced it well, but without his distinction, so that now we feel impelled to fasten a date upon her work, whereas his work rises above fashion and trend. Edward Wilson (1886-) has had a long and prolific career, the only one of the Pyle students still immersed in illustration. His rousing, flamboyant pictures for such

JESSIE WILLCOX SMITH
Child's Garden of Verses
Charles Scribner's Sons

EDWARD A. WILSON
Iron Men and Wooden Ships
Doubleday, Page and Company

73

books as *Treasure Island, Westward Ho!,* and *Last of the Mohicans* are fine examples of the romantic-adventure tradition. The most successful children's book of Thornton Oakley (1881-1955) was *Westward Ho!* and William Aylward (1875-1956) displayed his knowledge of ships and the sea in his excellent *Twenty Thousand Leagues Under the Sea.*

From the original Pyle students, the influence of the Brandywine tradition spread into wider circles, but mixed now with other influences as it reached the third and fourth generations. Harvey T. Dunn, George Harding, Thornton Oakley, W. J. Aylward, N. C. Wyeth, and Walter Everitt became well-known teachers as well as illustrators. Many of their students and students of their students have taught with the result that, a modified spirit of Pyle's mannerisms have found their way into American illustration. The Howard Pyle collection at the Wilmington Society of Fine Arts is still a mecca for art students, and Pyle first editions are collector's items.

HOWARD PYLE
Harper's Young People

74

A. B. FROST
Uncle Remus

CHAPTER 7

The American Accent

THE IMPETUS OF COMBINED TECHNOLOGICAL ADVANCE and increased craving for the printed word and picture that encouraged the Pyle tradition to shape itself and spread, gave the same opportunity to a host of waiting talents. No one suspected that the country was so rich in talent. It sprang into action almost overnight and in a short time formed one of the most accomplished schools of illustration in the world.

For it was a school that learned many lessons from the Old World and the Orient but still possessed an American tang and exuberance. It was not a regimented school; it embraced the widest variety of talents. But the American flavor permeated almost all of it.

Two handsome talents that represented extremes of viewpoint and technique were those of Edwin A. Abbey (1852-1911) and Arthur B. Frost (1851-1928). Abbey was the least American of the whole company; Frost as American as his own salty backcountry characters. Abbey, born and raised in Philadelphia and trained in its Academy of the Fine Arts, was spiritually an Englishman as he became later in actuality. He was a lover of costume, old ways, old things, a master of gesture and character, and a deeply sensitive and graceful pen draughtsman. Frost had a lively pen line too, but he was forthright and natural, with a zest for the quirks of human nature and the beauties and oddities of the natural world. He drew almost always with a twinkle in his

A. B. FROST
Uncle Remus

eye. Perhaps his masterpiece was the set of pictures for Joel Chandler Harris's *Uncle Remus,* a rare and definitive union of text and pictures. This has become an American classic. Its homely humor and penetrating caricature have never staled.

Frost never became one of a "school" but he had much in common with a fellow artist, Edward W. Kemble (1861-1933). They both loved the same friendly and humorous American types, the old fashioned American countryside, and the small town life that even then was changing and disappearing. Kemble had a homespun talent; his work was artless and without affectation — a natural, unsophisticated pictorial eye which was united to an untutored but ingratiating technique. Kemble was the first illustrator of Mark Twain's *Adventures of Huckleberry Finn.*

A. B. FROST
Uncle Remus

76

A. B. FROST
Uncle Remus

FREDERIC REMINGTON
Sketch

With Frost, Kemble, and Pyle, a fourth artist, Frederic Remington (1861-1909), made a quartet of salty, native picturemakers. Remington was the great pictorial reporter of the Far West. He came to it in the days of its last splendor, with the fading of the cowboy, the last pathetic belligerence of the Indian, and the ploughing of the great cattle ranges. He had a great feeling for the wiry men, Indian and white, who rode its prairies and hills. No one has celebrated the last frontier so well and so enduringly. Remington would never have considered himself a children's illustrator, yet tens of thousands of American boys have pored over his drawings with heart-thumping excitement. He was the father of a school of Wild-West picturemaking that has never lost its audience.

These four men did not stand alone. They were surrounded by a large circle of fertile and gifted artists, but they were central to a sudden burst of pictorial utterance that carried the tang and bite of the American accent. They were powerful agents in revealing us to ourselves and to the world. They were prime figures in what may have been called a *golden age* of American illustration. After a period of partial neglect, it is now time to celebrate their achievements. They have much to tell us about our sources.

EDWARD W. KEMBLE
Drawing in the author's collection

· MAE GERHARD
Unpublished Illustration

CHAPTER 8

Toward the Present

OF THE LARGE ARRAY OF EXCELLENT PICTUREMAKERS who appeared simultaneously with the rapid perfection of photoengraving, only a few bent their talents to the young. After all, talent alone, no matter how impressive, does not necessarily make an artist a first-rate children's illustrator. A special flair, probably beyond firm definition, is needed. Many artists must have been aware that they lacked the necessary sympathy with the child's world and interests. Some may have thought art for childhood was of minor importance. Others may have found adult illustration more demanding and remunerative. This must have been particularly so in the United States, where the spectacular growth of the weekly and monthly magazines attracted the gifted and ambitious. Excellent men like Edward Penfield, Albert Sterner, Andre Castaigne, Robert Blum, and Walter Appleton Clark seem to have given all their pictorial ideas to an adult audience. Even such a commanding figure as Charles Dana Gibson (1867-1944), whose pen drawings became accepted symbols of a whole generation, seems to have illustrated only two books which, from their titles, suggest that they were for children, *Witch Winnie's Mystery* (Dodd, 1891), and *People of Dickens* (Russell, 1897) — although, of course, many children pored over his pictures in such magazines as *Life, Tid-Bits, Century, Scribner's,* and *Harper,* and in the Gibson picture albums that were placed conspicuously on the parlor tables of many homes.

79

There were some excellent talents that spoke directly to children such as Palmer Cox, Peter Newell, Oliver Herford and Reginald Birch. Palmer Cox (1840-1924) is almost forgotten, but he gave delight to thousands of children and grown-ups for years, and his ingratiating and guileless humor can still be relished by those not encased in a crust of over-sophistication. His "Brownie" books are interesting examples of an innocent sense of fun that was less uncommon then than now. Peter Newell (1862-1924) and Oliver Herford (1863-1935) were more artful delineators; their humor was more subtle, and Herford in particular had an effortless wit that appealed to older minds. Both men drew with an engaging charm. Reginald Birch (1856-1943) carried the Victorian flavor into the new century, but his natural warmth and lack of affectation and technical trickery enabled him to avoid the tiresome cliches of his tradition and he deserved the popularity that he enjoyed for many years.

America was well served by its humorist illustrators in the early years of the century. Besides Cox, Newell, Frost, and Herford, two with special gifts were Walter Harrison Cady (1877-) and T. S. Sullivant (1854-1926). Cady created a pictorial domain of absurd bug life, pictures crammed with minute incidents and paraphernalia that enticed the eye to linger, return and discover. T. S. Sullivant's work appealed to both young and old. He was a delineator of the ridiculous; his human and animal forms were irresistible and inimitable.

PALMER COX
The Brownies at Home
Century Company

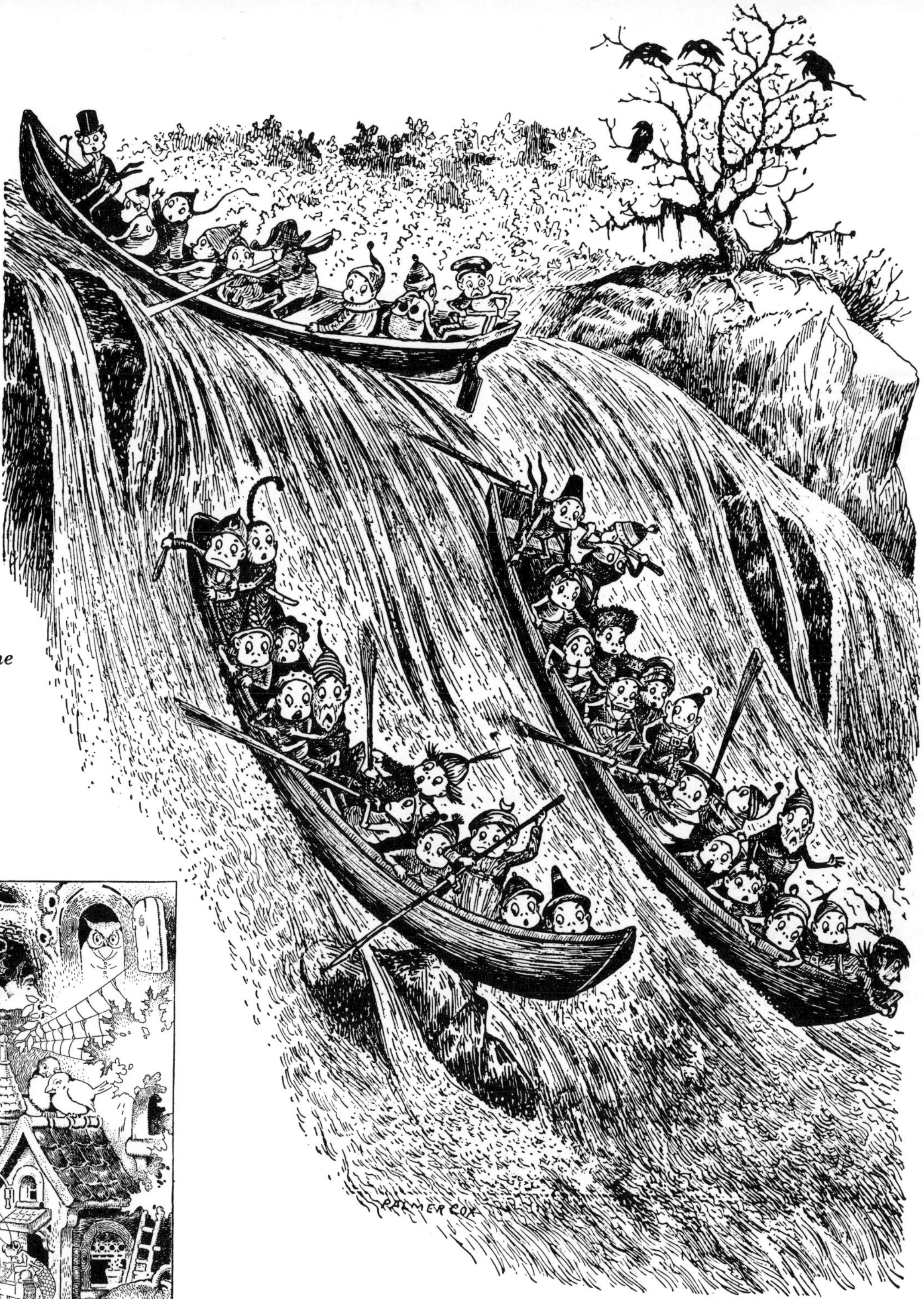

PALMER COX
The Brownies at Home
Century Company

WALTER HARRISON CADY
The Happy Chaps
St. Nicholas

81

A goodly portion of children's illustration was in the hands of the Howard Pyle students, but not all. There was by now a wide variety of talents in the field. Most of these illustrators were excellent picture-makers; but only a few were designers as well, interested in the entire book as a design unit. The halftone was in the ascendency, but there was still some demand for line cuts. Too often the pen drawings made for line cuts reflected the artist's desperate attempt to imitate the tonal range of the halftone and became fussy and overworked. Among the prominent artists in the field (and some of them were to remain active for several generations), were Ernest Thompson Seton, Dan Beard, Remington Schuyler, Everett Shinn, Willy Pogany, Wilfred Jones, Paul Honore, and Charles Falls.

C. B. FALLS
A.B.C. Book
Doubleday, Page and Company

82

Ernest Thompson Seton (1860-1946) and Dan Beard (1850-1941) were both writers as well as picturemakers and both were interested in nature and the life of the outdoors. Their pictures were always a supplement to the text but they were clear and factual line drawings that fulfilled their prime intent as visual clarifications of the text. Thompson Seton's books about animals like *The Trail of the Sandhill Stag, Lives of the Hunted,* and *Biography of a Grizzly,* were not only popular in their day but are still in demand. Remington Schuyler (1884-1955) had a masculine touch for the vigorous and picturesque side of American life and history. His work has been an excellent example of the American boy's adventure tradition, a sector of illustration that has attracted a large company of competent artists. Everett Shinn (1876-1953) trained in the old school of newspaper reportorial illustration, had the facility that came from that kind of youthful experience, but if he encountered the seamier side of life in his early days, it was translated into elegant brushwork and sophisticated drawing in his later pictures. Willy Pogany (1882-1955) brought from his native Hungary an opulent and often overworked sense of design, rich invention and great technical facility. A new note in American illustration, the involved decoration of his long series of books such as *Tannhauser, Magyar Fairy Tales,* and *Willy Pogany's Mother Goose,* now have great interest as period pieces. Wilfred Jones (1888-) has always been a pictorial designer. Every drawing of his has been conceived as a decorative area on a page and he should be credited with being among the earliest who strove to bring back good design to the book page.

Paul Honore (1885-1954) and Charles Falls (1874-1960) were almost the only book artists who were using the woodcut in the twenties. Both were excellent designers with a fine appreciation of letter forms and page layout and both were expert in the handling of strong, simple areas of flat color. Falls' *ABC Book* of 1923 was a landmark and Honore's series of decorative illustrations for several books of Charles Finger were unusual and provocative in their time.

World War I checked for a few years the expansion of book publishing; but by the time the post-war economic wheels were grinding again a younger generation of artists was entering the field — a larger group than ever before. Through the twenties this group grew rapidly, for the children's book field was beginning to ripen to its present remarkable development.

Such artists as Dorothy Lathrop, Robert Lawson, Donald Teague, Edward Shenton, Henry Pitz, Katherine Milhous, Boris Artzybasheff, Lynd Ward, Nura Ulreich, Mead Schaeffer, Helen Sewell, Wanda Gag, James Daugherty, Armstrong Sperry, Howard Sichel, Manning Lee, and Marguerite De Angeli were beginning their professional lives. It was a time when the first sniff of change was in the air, a change that would not become clearly apparent until the next decade.

KATHERINE MILHOUS
With Bells On
Charles Scribner's Sons

SHEILAH BECKETT

EDWARD SHENTON
Best in Children's Books
Nelson Doubleday, Inc.

BORIS ARTZYBASHEFF
Poor Shaydullah
Macmillan

VALENTI ANGELO
Golden Gate
Viking Press

JAMES DAUGHERTY
Knickerbocker's History of New York
Doubleday, Doran and Company

Books put together by rote was the general rule. Pictures, usually halftones made from oil and wash drawings, were *tipped* or glued in by hand, adjacent to their proper text. There was a great textural discrepancy between the shiny surface of the halftone and the blotter-like consistency of the text pages. Little care was spent upon proper type selection or in the spacing of it. The world of the trade book had scarcely heard of the word design.

Undoubtedly, both the publisher and the artist — and public too — were still in a glow of wonder over the perfection of the halftone. For the first time tonal pictures were being reproduced quickly and fairly cheaply. Halftones were fashionable. There was little refreshing contact with the publishing of Europe. British books, it is true, were imported in large numbers, especially the large, impressive *gift book* editions; but British book design was not much better than American, in spite of a lingering of the William Morris ideal. Still, among a group of lesser gifts, every year England sent us the latest editions of two exceptional men: Arthur Rackham and Edmund Dulac. Rackham's work was English to the core; the deep down, fanciful, and poetic side of the English that is shy about exhibiting itself. Dulac was eclectic and cosmopolitan, a splendid designer and natural colorist. These two artists tend to be waved away with faint praise today but they are still the best of their kinds, and many of their books escaped the curse of poor design. The early editions of Dulac's *Bells* and *The Kingdom of the Pearl* and Rackman's *Cinderella* need no apologies. They are well designed books. Until the twenties, the only foreign influence of note, and it was a great one, was that of the English book.

Many different minds and organizations began sincere and persistent work for the betterment of children's books before the turn of

LYND WARD
The Canadian Story
Farrar, Straus and Company

the century. The first children's room was opened in a free library as late as 1893. In 1896, Anne Carroll Moore was appointed children's librarian at the Pratt Institute Free Library in Brooklyn, New York, and began her aggressive, lifelong career as a champion of children's books of excellence. She edited the first children's book column in the *New York Herald Tribune* and her *Three Owls* was one of the first books to discuss American writing and art for children. Children's book columns and reviews of children's books have now spread to many newspapers throughout the country and to quite a few magazines. Children's book rooms in the libraries and children's book departments in bookstores are now taken for granted, but they were new things up until the twenties.

One of the most powerful forces behind the growth of the children's book has been the growing group of children's book editors. When the Macmillan Company in New York City created a children's book department in 1919 and made Louise Seaman its editor, the start was made. Three years later, May Massee was appointed to the same position at Doubleday, Doran and Company. It was fortunate that these two early positions were filled by women of exceptional energy, taste and conviction, for their success led many publishers to follow their example. Today, the now enlarged company of children's book editors is remarkably astute and aware. Their abilities vary, of course, but the liveliness and competitiveness of the field weeds out the incompetents.

The field was studded with personalities. When, in 1916, Bertha E. Mahony opened the Bookshop for Boys and Girls in Boston, it was the beginning of a chain of accomplishments. The shop was stocked with the most interesting books from all over the world, — a catalog was written which was so popular that it became an annual and then a semi-annual review. Finally, in 1924, it turned into the well-known *Horn Book* which regularly devoted all its space to the world of children's books. This, in turn, led to the important "who's who" of children's illustrators, *Contemporary Illustrators of Children's Books,* published in 1930. An expanded volume, *Illustrators of Children's Books,* was published in 1947, followed by *Illustrators of Children's Books 1946-1956.*

Aside from the growing literature on children's books, other activities have multiplied. In 1918, the first Children's Book Week was launched by New York librarians and editors and it has become an annual event of increasing importance. It has spread from city to city and is now a truly national event; a period of exhibitions, meetings, and appraisals of the year's output of children's books. The annual convention of the American Library Association and the numerous regional meetings of librarians devote a considerable amount of time to children. There are now courses on children's literature in many colleges. Each year two important medals are awarded, the Newbery, for distinguished writing, and the Caldecott for an outstanding picture book. Frederic Melcher, who has done many things for the book field, had an important part in creating these two awards.

The formation of the Junior Literary Guild, in 1929, was an important factor in increasing the distribution of children's books. Since then, other book clubs have come into the field with varying degrees of success.

The American Institute of Graphic Arts assembled its first exhibition of "The Fifty Books of the Year" in 1923. It jolted many American publishers into a consciousness of what fine bookmaking could be and opened their eyes to the considerable number of well-designed books that were already being produced. This exhibition is now an annual event and a spur toward high standards of design and workmanship.

Looking back now, we can see that a strong tide of interest in children's books had been set in motion early in this century. It was running in strength by the thirties, and the most important reason for its power was the large company of illustrators and designers—men and women of gifts and enterprise who had thrown themselves into a congenial and devoted task. Capable illustrators were pouring out of the art schools now, and undoubtedly one of the reasons for the richness of talent that was appearing was the fertilizing effect of America's melting pot. The younger artists came from all walks of life, a great variety of regional backgrounds, and a diversity of racial strains. Just to name some of our native-born artists is to call up a kaleidoscopic image of races and cultures: Woodi Ishmael, Valenti Angelo, Frederick Chapman, William Pene Du Bois, Harold Von Schmidt, Elinore Blaisdell, John McCloskey, Wanda Gag, Rudolf Freund, Paul Honore, Nils Hogner, Paul Bransom, Paul Lantz, Lois Lenski, and Irene Haas. Add to this a battalion of foreign artists, men and women of high reputation in their own countries, who have been attracted by the opportunities of America—illustrators like the D'Aulaires, Fritz Kredel, Rafaello Busoni, Roger Duvoisin, Fritz Eichenberg, Feodor Rojankovsky, Kate Seredy, Gustaf Tenggren, and Nicolas Mordvinoff—and we can understand the multi-faceted character of the American children's book.

DR. SEUSS
The Sneetches and Other Stories
Random House

HENRY C. PITZ
With Might and Main
Alfred A. Knopf

89

It is impossible to fence in this upsurge in children's books with precision, but certainly it has been in full flow for more than thirty years. Even the Second World War did little to diminish it. It seems that every possible subject and every possible method of graphic expression has been explored, and yet there appears to be no signs of slackening. Every yard of the earth's surface has been searched for material, the skies above, and the waters beneath. Innumerable little native boys and girls from every race, clan, and tribe have had their stories told. Every *beastie* from the animal kingdom has been given speech, thought, and frequently a sense of humor, and has been put between the covers of a book. There seems to be no compartment of the natural world that has not been explained and pictured. There are books describing how things function, what makes things go, and how to make practically anything that can be made.

Every size, shape, format, page arrangement and binding has been tried. Books not only open; they have been made to pop up, pull out, fold, come apart, make noises, and draw out like an accordion. Some have come with synthetic *fur* for stroking fingers. American inventiveness has had a field day.

The wildest and most absurd experiments seem to have simmered down. After all, the editors work in an atmosphere of sharp competition and there is temptation to reach for extremes and novelties. The resources of art modernism hold out a natural invitation and some excellent pictorial effects have come from that direction — and some silly ones too. Up-to-dateness is a trivial ideal to pursue.

During the past three decades or more, there have been many artists who have made important contributions to the art of children's books. The early decorated books of Boris Artzybasheff (1899-) brought a new and exciting element into book design. Highly patterned in strong black and white contrasts, his pictures dazzled and startled the eye. Artists and connoisseurs collected such little gems as *Creatures* and *Fairy Shoemaker*. He was less successful with children, however, for many were bewildered by his powerful patterns. But his *Seven Simeons* was a masterpiece that captured all audiences.

Some years later, a fellow Russian émigré, Feodor Rojankovsky (1891-) sounded another fresh but different note with his drawings, so superb in tactile values that children imagined they could feel the furry backs of his animals. His *Tall Book of Mother Goose* and *Tall Book of*

90

Nursery Tales vitalized these much-illustrated texts. These books were planned by the Artists and Writers Guild, an organization that has been responsible for a great number of outstanding works. They have offered opportunities for a group of fine illustrators, including Gustaf Tenggren, Cornelius De Witt, Tibor Gergely and Beth and Joseph Krush. They have used the beautifully rendered, factual drawings of Rudolf Freund and Harry McNaught and the splendidly imaginative paintings of the Provensens. Many fine ideas for the content and format of these books were brought from France by Georges Duplaix and, since his retirement, have been carried on by Lucille Ogle.

GUSTAF TENGGREN
Tenggren's Story Book
Simon and Schuster

FEODOR ROJANKOVSKY
The Tall Mother Goose
Harper and Brothers

91

A third Russian artist of distinction who has come to us is Nicolas Mordvinoff (1911-). He has a long list of books to his credit, including a recent Caldecott winner, *Finders Keepers*. Two of his finest sets of illustrations, quite different from his recent drawings, were in the first two of his books printed in this country, *Pepe Was The Saddest Bird* and *The Ship of Flame*. A few years ago, *The Borrowers* attracted a great deal of attention, and focused attention upon the illustrators, the husband and wife team of Beth (1918-) and Joe Krush (1918-). These fine artists had been working quietly for years, turning out book after book of high excellence and receiving too little credit for the beauty and charm of their work. Charm is in bad odor with the critics, but it is a chance-given gift that has always exerted a curious power and always will. Illustrators like Garth Williams, Mary Chalmers, Edward Ardizzone, Ludwig Bemelmans, Leonard Weisgard, and a few others have it in abundance.

NICOLAS MORDVINOFF
Pepe Was the Saddest Bird
Alfred A. Knopf

92

LEONARD WEISGARD
Charles Scribner's Sons

RICHARD FLOETHE
If I Were Captain
Charles Scribner's Sons

The woodcut has been revived for children's books with great vigor and distinction by Antonio Frasconi (1919-). Frasconi is not only an unusually able picturemaker and designer, but he seems to have an innate gift for conveying ideas to children in immediate and captivating pictorial terms. A small school of woodcut illustrators have been ignited by his example, including his able wife, Leona Pierce. Sometimes using the linoleum cut, but more often simulating it with the pen line, Joseph Low (1911-) has evolved a personal and provocative style compounded from elements of numerous older cultures and a judicious mixture of modernism. Low has love for all cultures and great skill with letter forms and his page designs are always a delight. At the other extreme from the bold and simple statements of this school, is the work of the highly skilled men who delineate the intricate structure of nature — the semi-scientific depictors of birds, fish, flowers, crystals — the whole gamut of nature's forms. Perhaps the most accomplished of this group is Rudolf Freund, whose large color books on animals, flowers, snakes and butterflies are works of art as well as being scientifically accurate.

MARCIA BROWN
Woodcut illustrating for
"Once a Mouse"
Charles Scribner's Sons

LEONA PIERCE
Woodcut for "Who Likes the Sun?"
Harcourt, Brace and World

ANTONIO FRASCONI
*Woodcut Illustration for
"The Snow and the Sun,"
Harcourt, Brace and World*

95

Publishers are fond of publishing books in series, and a great many of these have appeared in recent years, built around a variety of themes. The American historical theme has been a popular one and the most conspicuous group built around it has been the "Landmark" series. It is notable for its size, variety, and high standard of text and pictures. A long list of artists, including Edward Wilson, Norman Price, Jacob Landau, Isa Barnett, William Sharp, Aldren Watson, and John O'Hara Cosgrave have contributed to it.

A series that was particularly well designed and printed was the "Evergreen" series of classic children's tales, published by the Limited Editions Club. It was an artistic success, but scarcely a financial one, for children usually showed their love for a book by wearing it out rapidly and few parents could afford the expense of these finely produced books. They are now collector's items with their illustrations by Edy Legrand, Ervine Metzl, Malcolm Cameron, Fritz Eichenberg, Sylvain Sauvage, Edward Shenton, and Robert Lawson.

In the historical field, *American Heritage* is now sponsoring a splendid series, well planned and largely illustrated with contemporary documentary material, which has helped to remind us of the work of some of our artists of the past. In the area of the children's imaginative tests, the "Golden Book" series of Simon and Schuster is still of commanding importance. The recent work of the Provensens, Alice (1918-) and Martin (1916-) in books like *The Iliad, The Odyssey,* and *Myths and Legends* is outstanding.

J. P. MILLER
The Wonderful House
Golden Press

96

ROGER DUVOISIN
Veronica
Alfred A. Knopf

An interesting factor in this mushroom growth of children's books has been the increase in the single author-artist. Of course, this combination is not new. Such people as Howard Pyle and Beatrix Potter had both written and illustrated their own books. But the author-artist is yearly becoming more common. The illustrator is always close to the written word, of course, and close contact usually results in a kind of literary education for him. And it must be confessed that when he looks at the scanty texts that he is asked to picture and the sometimes rich royalties that they draw, he is prompted to think, "I could do this. I'll try it." He often does and sometimes succeeds quite well. A great many fine books have resulted from this combination, as for example the works of Marguerite De Angelo, Wanda Gag, William Pene Du Bois, Grace Paull, James Daugherty, Kate Seredy, Donald E. Cook, Reiner Zimnik, Roger Duvoisin, Robert McCloskey, Lois Lenski, Will James, Holling C. Holling, Katherine Milhous, and others.

The illustrators have drawn, sometimes written, and a smaller group have even taught. Being creatively engaged in the field, such teachers have brought an air of professionalism to the art school and exacted higher standards. The quality of illustration students' work went up considerably in the period of about 1930 to 1950, many gifted recruits entered professional life from such schools as Pratt Institute, the Philadelphia Museum College of Art, and the Rhode Island School of Design.

The period was active, restless and bubbling with new ideas; a time of triumphs and mistakes; a time of effort and great stimulation; a time of interesting and provocative personalities. Those who took part in it will always remember the battles, the defeats, the victories, the sense of being part of something worthwhile; but looking backward now the peaks are more visible than the valleys.

REINER ZIMNIK
Drummers of Dreams
Faber and Faber

CHAPTER **9**

Matters Ponderable and Imponderable

IF ONE HAS MADE AT LEAST A BRIEF SURVEY of the children's books of the past and has explored a reasonable segment of the present-day output, a store of uncatalogued impressions will have accumulated in the mind. Will this store of impressions be useful and beneficial? Almost certainly, yes. Will it reveal the secret of writing and picturing a great children's book? No—unless the secret is already part of one's natural endowments.

All the arts are crowded with relentless seekers after the secret of creation. Most people search for it in the wrong places. It is found within, although sometimes a circumstance from without discloses the inner power. Thousands of good minds have talked or written about this central mystery. In fact, it is the tantalizing core around which revolves most of the literary, musical, dramatic and artistic criticism of the ages, an enormous monument of comment available to all. But nowhere is there a transmissible formula for guaranteed creation. All this is conversation—delightful, informative conversation. The secret reveals itself to genius; it may disclose itself through study, constant practice, and buoyant persistence; but if and when it appears, it will not show itself in the shape of a recipe. Rather, it will make itself felt as a permeating understanding, an inner realization and consciousness of power that will be apprehended by the intuition.

Creation operates on many levels and most children's books are written and illustrated by craftsmen whose modest creative endowments have been sharpened and focused by much practice and the use of intelligence. That is the common path, with rewards for the successful, who are always a minority.

The editors of children's books know that the world is filled with writers and artists-to-be. They receive hundreds of manuscripts, book dummies and sets of pictures every year. Only a few see publication, and almost always these need to be revised and worked over with the experienced help of the editors. This condition is not peculiar to the children's book world. It is repeated in other fields of the arts for commerce.

Why is so much hopeful material unusable? For two conspicuous reasons: *the aspirants know too little about themselves and too little about the field in which they hope to operate.* The reasons for wishing to rush into print are often insufficient. There are many mothers who captivate their small ones by invented tales and who are ambitious for a larger audience. But a mother's loving voice to her own children can do things that cold print cannot do to strange children.

Many have looked at a current crop of children's books (particularly the poorer ones); and, unimpressed by a scant few hundred words of text and some fumbled drawings (hiding behind the label of modernism), have said to themselves, "There isn't much to this — I could do better." They may be right but usually they aren't — and being a little better than mediocre isn't enough anyway. If publishers are weak enough to print mediocre books — and they do — they will take them from the hands of professionals. It is true that a few children's books have come from authors or illustrators who have made a one-or-two-time invasion of the field; but the great majority are produced by those who have made a serious and continuous investment of time and effort in this sphere. If one plans merely a flying sortie into this world, the chances of success are remote — and rightly so. One should feel genuinely drawn toward this world, and conscious of having something to contribute to it.

A rigid examination of one's motives, talents, knowledge and resources is a good starting place. Then there is the factual, mechanical side of publishing that so few novices know anything about. It helps greatly to present a manuscript and drawings in a workmanlike way, so that the editors are conscious that they are dealing with someone who can speak their language. The following chapters are an introduction to that area, but a reading of them is not enough. They must be put into practice until assimilated. Trying to learn the fundamental intricacies of book publication should drive home the conviction that a price of effort and time must be paid in order to enter a field which is, after all, highly competitive.

Although hastiness and superficiality deserve to be discouraged, it would be wrong to give the impression that nothing short of devoting every waking hour to the task has any chance of success. There are many professional authors and artists in the field who, immersed in other duties, only devote a portion of their time to children's books. One of the most successful of today's author-artists has raised a family of five children; her numerous and popular books have not hampered her from being a complete wife and mother. But she has always had more than normal energy and will.

It is in getting acquainted with the books of the past and the present that a feel for subject, method and atmosphere can be built up. Examining the books of the present should develop a sense of the climate of the moment; reviewing those of the past should reveal that trend has followed trend; and the present is only a brief interval in an endless series of rhythms. It is wise and often necessary to conform to the fashions of the moment, but not to become a captive of them. Recognizing what is popular, however necessary, is no great feat; but sensing what is going to become popular requires unusual powers, and they cannot be bought. In fact, any time a tendency is plain for everyone to see, we may conclude that it is past its peak and in retreat. Wherever there is a strong trend, look for its opposite to appear.

The small talent follows trends; the strong talent makes its own. It is the strong talents that have created the little islands of permanence in the sea of tidal fashions. *Alice in Wonderland, The Wind in the Willows,* Howard Pyle's tales and pictures, *The Wizard of Oz,* and *Struwwelpeter* are still nourishing young minds. Mother Goose, Hans Christian Andersen, and the Brothers Grimm are still there. *Robinson Crusoe, Gulliver's Travels* and *Treasure Island,* have not faded. At the moment a goodly number of Victorian favorites, fantasy particularly, are being reprinted to satisfy a demand. Undoubtedly, this is a countercurrent moving against a too-insistent tide of factual content, of modern *chic* gone to excess, of overzealous smartness.

The novice immersing himself in the world of children's literature can saturate himself with awareness if he is receptive. It will sensitize him not merely to factual knowledge but to the sense of magic and the improbable, to atmosphere, to the weight and resilience of words, to the delight of color and line, to a heightened appetite for the visible world. These are the things that count. If he is looking only for answers that can be stated on a graph, a prescription, or in a neat sum, that is all he will get. There are a certain number of these in the children's world, which should be noted and taken for what they are, possible straws in a wind. As a sole diet they are suitable only for pedants. The writing and picturing of children's books is an art, no matter how humble it may be at times. Those who practice this art need sharpened perceptions, deepened awareness, and increased skills, none of which come out of a bottle.

ERIK BLEGVAD
"I'm Hiding"
Harcourt, Brace and Company

PART II. TECHNIQUE AND PRODUCTION

HILARY KNIGHT
Beloved Tales
Golden Press

MARY VILLAREJO
The Art Fair
Alfred A. Knopf

CHAPTER **10**

The Illustrator in the Children's World

THE YOUNG ILLUSTRATOR WHO STEPS into the children's world, hopeful perhaps of making pictures for it, should know by the feeling in his bones whether he belongs or not. He may feel bewildered and inadequate, he may discern that there is a great deal to be learned, but he should be able to sense whether he is attracted or repelled. Unless he feels drawn toward it and believes he has something to give it, he should turn his back and seek other fields. There are always those who come to it for success and money. These are certainly not unworthy motives but, by themselves, they are not enough. The necessary ingredients of sympathy and devotion are missing.

By and large, the illustrators of children's books, be their talents large or small, are a group who practice the thing they love. The material rewards are usually much greater in other fields; but they prefer the freedom, the inviting subject matter, the sense of accomplishment, and the lift of a responsive audience. There is an atmosphere of relative permanence about it too, and the pressures of commercialism are not too oppressive.

It also has its problems, however, and no artist can solve them by giving way to his own whims alone. Children are both predictable and unpredictable, and so their artists have to be flexible but, at the same time, aware of basic appetites and tendencies. After all, the making of pictures for children is not a new art. The accumulated experience of

105

the many gifted and intelligent persons who have worked in the field provides a treasury of valuable information for the newcomer.

No one — artist, writer, editor, or librarian — can become involved in the world of children's books for very long without discovering that the age span of childhood has been carved into convenient segments. On the surface, it would almost seem that every few years the child should move from one compartment to another, until he escapes into adulthood. Remember, though, age groups are arbitrary — an artificial system imposed upon the free-moving growth of childhood by adults for convenience of planning and discussion. One category blends into another imperceptibly. Children of the same age can be above or below their expected categories, or may lap over into several. The classifications are no more than a rough measuring scale, which can be very useful but is sometimes abused.

It is believed that most children show a desire to learn to read about the age of six and that they show an interest in books before the reading age, if there are pictures to be looked at or if a friendly voice will read to them; so children's books can appeal to children one to three years of age.

THE PICTUREBOOK AGE

The book for the youngest age must be, of course, a picture book, although a few simple sentences accompany the pictures. It is for a little creature opening his eyes to a fresh and bewildering world, and the pictures must help to set that world in order. The pictorial language is a new thing too, so the pictures will be simple and direct, identifying familiar things: a chair, a cat, a spoon, ball, or flower. This is the time of the first wonder and the earliest explorations. The child is discovering himself, his family, his home, the common objects of life, his pets, the warmth of the sun, the wind, the skies. This should be exciting material for any artist, but uncondescending simplicity of presentation is an ability not given to everyone.

The pictures (and text) must be presented with knowing simplicity — a thought, a shape at a time. The child's attention span is very short, from seconds to a few minutes; so the book must be a matter of few and uncluttered pages. The text should be brief; it is only a guide for the adult's voice. The pictures should be large and abundant, in color if possible, and treated with simple realism. Line seems to be a pictorial convention easily grasped by children; their own early drawings will be expressed wholly or largely by line. Finally, the book should be sturdy. It may be handled lovingly but clumsily for a long time — chewed, tossed and torn.

The next age bracket is from three to five, an age when children have become more familiar with pictures and may even be able to read a line or two. But the text is still an accompaniment to the all-important pictures. The successful books written and illustrated for this age often seem absurdly simple and trivial to some adult minds. Their simplicity, however, is deceptive. They require a special understanding, the rare knack of being able to think as a young child. The theme may seem slight, but it must spring from a child's enlarging interest. It must be an answer to a budding question, an appealing, reassuring answer. The material comes out of the child's own small world. It will be pictured simply, convincingly and with a light touch.

The attention span has now lengthened to ten, fifteen, perhaps twenty minutes; so the book is a bit longer, very likely from thirty-two to forty-eight pages. This book will still be taking punishment and, therefore, its format should be sturdy.

Although the text is a minor part of the book for this age group, many authors forget that it should be suitable for reading out loud. The words should not only be simple and understandable to the child; they should fall easily and rhythmically from the lips. In fact, the success or failure of any of these books is dependent upon the effectiveness of the reading.

LEARNING TO READ

Children at the *beginning to read* age of about six to eight, are developing rapidly. They are not only beginning to read, but have found out a multitude of things about the world in which they live. They are going to school and making the adjustment from being the center of attention to being one of many. They still need reassurance and guardianship, but also encouragement toward independence.

Now for the first time, a book must take one of two possible paths to reach the child. He can read, it is true, but only in a very limited way — and a book intended for self-reading must work within those limits. The child's awareness of the world has far outdistanced his reading ability. He is eager to add to his knowledge through books that must be read to him; so the text now becomes of much greater importance. But there must be no indecision as to whether the purpose is to read or be read to.

The attention span is constantly increasing, and in the *to be read to* category the book may be quite long. A book of over a hundred pages can be read in installments. Plot, action, and characterization become important, with spirit, movement, and clarity in the pictures.

The book *to be read by the child* must be shorter, its vocabulary adjusted to the age group, its sentences short but rhythmic. The text should be set in 14-16- or 18-point type, or even larger. The best books of this class should contain excellent page design, a beautiful and satisfying relationship between the letter forms and the pictorial images.

THE MOST IMPORTANT READING AGE

The years between nine and twelve are usually considered the major reading ages. The child who has formed the habit of reading becomes ravenous for the printed word and picture. Later, studies, games and social activities may diminish this ardor; but for a while it is a greedy and expansive time of immersion and absorption in books. Anything — all things — can be of interest. There will be many situations or facts that will be beyond his intellectual or emotional capacities for the time being, but he will be curious about them nevertheless. It is a time for imaginative roving and a sharp appetite for facts, too. Daydreams and a passion for minute, concrete knowledge go hand in hand. This is the age when the sexes begin to pull apart. Many, many books interest both sexes equally; but there is also a necessity for the *girl's book* and the *boy's book,* each usually rejected by the other sex.

Illustrations for this age are more frequently printed in black and white than in color, but this is merely because of cost. The pictures may be both imaginative and sharply factual. This is the age when the boy is interested in detailed knowledge. He often knows more about cars, tools, airplanes, weapons and such things than his parents. He expects accuracy in his pictures and is only too eager to expose a careless illustrator's shortcomings. The well-designed book — jacket, binding, typography, picture pages — is important to an age that is becoming conscious of good planning and skillful execution. The illustrator, like the writer, must have a feeling for his audience, neither below or above them, but *with* them.

TOWARDS ADULTHOOD

The last age group to be considered is the "teen age." This group, of course, is trying to turn its back on childhood, with varying degrees of success, and is reaching toward adulthood. Its books should face toward adulthood too, perhaps being just a little out of reach. Better to be ahead of the "teenager" than behind him.

Some will have a beginning appreciation of style in prose and pictures. Characterization must be better than paper-thin. Problems, plots, and situations must have depth. Force, vigor, and action are eagerly absorbed qualities. The "teenager" must not find only himself in the narrative but adults too. In fact, this is the age when many prefer to read adult books. Adult classics now begin to come into their own; every year some of them are reprinted and reillustrated for a new audience. It is hard to place boundaries on the subject matter for this age. Events of the modern world, any of the many fascinating aspects of science, the lives of great and interesting people, information about what makes things run and how to construct a wide variety of objects, are some of the kinds of material that go into these near-adult books.

Again, the illustrator must have bounce and elasticity in his work and a high regard for the facts of the matter. He is facing an alert audience that is keenly perceptive of many things and usually more sharply critical than adults. The illustrator is forced to know his subject and have reasons for everything he does.

The illustrator cannot hope to be successful in the children's book field unless he is knowledgeable about and sympathetic with at least one of these groups. Some artists have these qualities instinctively; others can cultivate them. To get a feel of what kind of pictures appeal to what ages, he must immerse himself in what has been done and what is being done. He should spend a good deal of time in the children's rooms of libraries and bookstores, examining all the picture books that come to hand, evaluating, remembering, questioning, enjoying. Gradually the mass of evidence will arrange itself; certain qualities will become understandable; a *feel* for the child public and its various strata will develop. At the same time, the illustrator must study the *appearance* of children at various ages; he must draw them with reasonable confidence. Some of this knowledge will come from the books he has been examining; he will study the way other illustrators deal with the problem. But better than that he will be observing and drawing children themselves.

OBSERVING CHILDREN

Continued observation and drawing of children can be one of the most revealing segments of an illustrator's education. Drawing children does not necessarily consist in hiring and coaxing children to pose quietly in a studio, although that can be part of the program. Children are best studied when they are not self-conscious, when they are moving, playing, and absorbed in themselves. That means stalking them in the playgrounds, schoolyards, parks, back yards and streets. It often means sketching surreptitiously, using any dodge that promises concealment of one's purpose, such as drawing behind an opened newspaper. It means learning a calligraphic language that will seize only the essential masses and lines. It means the willingness to take what chance offers; the ability to grasp moments, scraps of an action, parts of a figure, hints of an attitude.

In fact, for this rapid jotting, one or the other of two procedures should be followed. First, a few essential and telling lines should be used to delineate a given action; as the action changes the jotting should be abandoned, incomplete as it may be, for the next phase of action. This results in page after page of partial and tentative statements—bits and scraps of drawings. But with practice those hasty lines become more and more expressive and meaningful and, finally, out of accumulated experience, the knowledge to complete those quick notes will be forthcoming. Second, one can jot down the beginning of an action and as it changes, tear one's eyes away from the moving figure and complete the sketch from memory. Both of these methods should be practiced and, as time goes on, the visual memory will be strengthened to retain a large part of the movements that have passed before the eyes. Of course the methods and practice of drawing children in their natural poses, may and should be expanded to include any or all living creatures and the whole natural world.

The juvenile illustrator may well consider children his major motif but they move in a world crowded with other beings and other forms. A common criticism aimed at some children's illustrators is that they cannot depict convincing grownups, not to mention the surrounding paraphernalia of life, buildings, furniture, trees, animals, automobiles —the whole endless list. The children's illustrator may consider himself a specialist but he must not appear noticeably ignorant of the world in which children live.

110

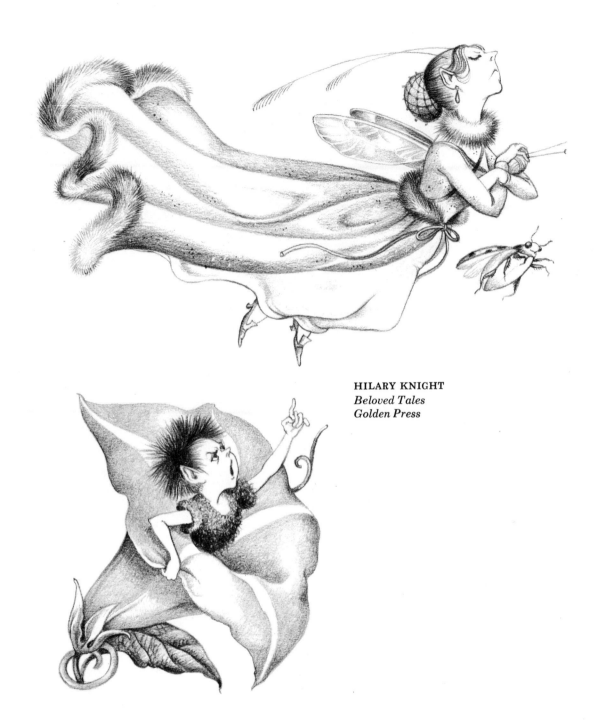

HILARY KNIGHT
Beloved Tales
Golden Press

111

TIBOR GERGELY
A Day in the Jungle
Artists and Writers Guild
Simon and Schuster

TIBOR GERGELY
A Day in the Jungle
Artists and Writers Guild
Simon and Schuster

WALT DISNEY
Walt Disney's Story Land
Golden Press

WILLIAM DUGAN
Old Friends and Lasting Favorites
Golden Press

115

J. P. MILLER
The Wonderful House
Golden Press

RICHARD SCARRY
Beloved Tales
Golden Press

MURRAY TINKLEMAN
Who Says Hoo?
Golden Press

LILIAN OBLIGADO
Beloved Tales
Golden Press

119

EDWARD SOREL
Gwendolyn, the Miracle Hen
Golden Press

GUSTAF TENGGREN
Farm Stories
Simon and Schuster

FEODOR ROJANKOVSKY
The Tall Book of Mother Goose
Harper and Brothers

FEODOR ROJANKOVSKY
The Tall Book of Mother Goose
Harper and Brothers

ELOISE WILKIN
Old Friends and Lasting Favorites
Golden Press

126

GORDON LAITE
Beloved Tales
Golden Press

NICOLAS MORDVINOFF

Just So Stories
Doubleday and Company, Inc.

LOWELL HESS
Old Friends and Lasting Favorites
Golden Press

128

MAE GERHARD
Old Friends and Lasting Favorites
Golden Press

GORDON LAITE
Old Friends and Lasting Favorites
Golden Press

ARTHUR SINGER
The Giant Golden Book of Birds
Golden Press

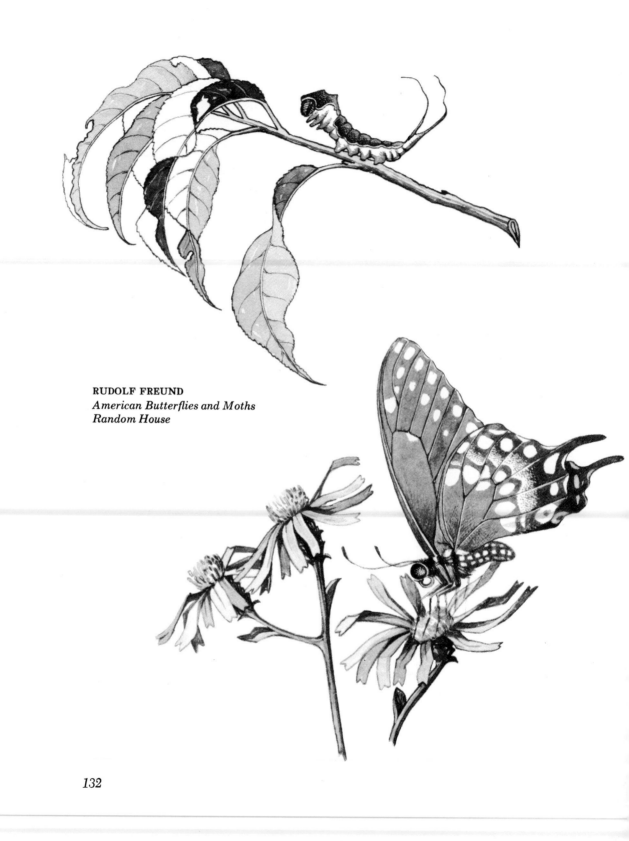

RUDOLF FREUND
American Butterflies and Moths
Random House

132

HARRY MCNAUGHT
The Golden Book of Science
Golden Press

133

MAE GERHARD
Old Friends and Lasting Favorites
Golden Press

WILLIAM DUGAN
Old Friends and Lasting Favorites
Golden Press

LEONARD WEISGARD
The Secret River
Charles Scribner's Sons

CHAPTER **11**

The Structure of the Book

BOOKS HAVE AN ANATOMY OF THEIR OWN, of which the intelligent designer or illustrator must have a grasp. The basic structure of the book imposes conditions upon its design, and since illustrations are part of the design they must adapt themselves to its functions. The book illustrator is, among other things, a technician conversant not only with the techniques of picturemaking but of book format.

The materials that go into bookmaking and the way they are put together must be understood: paper (its texture, color, thickness, receptivity to ink, and degree of opacity); binding materials (linen and synthetic cloths, paper, and cardboard); type (the customary book faces and the display faces used for jackets and title pages).

If anyone should be asked the trick question, "How many pages are in a book?" the answer, or lack of one, will instantly indicate if there is a grasp of the first fundamentals of book structure. The answer is, "Any number of pages divisible by FOUR." The only exceptions are the spiral of loose-leaf books, in which case the page number is divisible by two.

The basic unit of a book is a sheet of paper folded down the middle, making a unit of four pages. The next larger is a group of such folded sheets, usually four, eight or sixteen, slipped inside one another, making a small book-like form of sixteen, thirty-two or sixty-four pages. This larger unit is called a signature. These signatures can

135

vary in the number of sheets and pages they contain, although, of course, the total number must always be a multiple of four. In common practice, the usual page numbers are multiples of sixteen: thirty-two, forty-eight, sixty-four and so on. Finally, the total number of signatures, placed side by side in their proper order and bound, form the book as a whole.

The usual signature, folded and trimmed, is made up of a large single sheet or portion of a single sheet, which passes through the printing press to receive impressions on one side and is then turned over and passes through again to receive impressions on its other side. The printed sheets then pass on to a machine that folds and trims them into the signature form.

Although the paperback book now accounts for a large part of the total publishing output, the children's book is still almost entirely hardback or *case* bound. This entails a rather expensive binding process. The assembled signatures are pressed together, sewn together at the folded edges, and those edges are glued to a linen band. Meanwhile the *case* has been prepared: a front and back panel of press-board covered with linen or plastic cloth, with the space between the panels (the spine or shelfback, representing the thickness of the book) consisting sometimes only of the covering fabric and in some cases backed by flexible material. The united signatures are slipped into the case and the linen tabs of the signatures are glued to the inside panels of the pressboard. Finally, paper sheets called end papers, are glued over the inside of the casing panels to hide the linen joinings and to give the book a neat appearance.

The minor details of printing and binding a book are usually of slight importance to the illustrator and designer. Often, however, these details and the many ramifications of the process interest and fascinate the inquiring mind. A visit to a publishing plant is certain to clarify and imprint the essentials of the process in the mind.

Although not a part of the book proper, an adjunct of almost all case-bound books today is the book jacket. This is a sheet of paper printed with title, author's name, legends, and accompanied usually by some pictorial or decorative design. It is wrapped around the book with projecting flaps tucked inside the covers. The jacket is one of the illustrator's and designer's concerns.

GERALD ROSE
Wrap-around book-jacket for
"Old Winkle and the Seagulls"
Faber and Faber

Looking at the completed book from the outside, and opening it page by page, we can consider each item and what it means to the illustrator and designer.

THE BOOK JACKET

The book jacket began as a sheet of paper wrapped around the covers of the book to protect them from soil and handling. Today it is an important design piece in the make-up of the book. Its advertising possibilities are used to the utmost, and it can be regarded as a complex problem of package design. It must appeal at a reasonable distance through its colors and forms. It must convey legibly and directly the message of its title and author, and should project the purpose of its contents.

Besides this, there are mechanical restrictions of the jacket's shape and printing character. First of all, the jacket area to be designed divides itself into two or sometimes three panels. There is always the face; that is, the front which faces us as the closed book lies on the table. To its left, along the bound edge of the book, lies the narrow panel called the spine, shelfback or backbone. Sometimes the back cover of the jacket is included in the design area. This happens more frequently with children's books than with other types. More often it is given over to advertising copy and is not the concern of the artist.

Although these two or three panels should be designed as a unit, each panel has its own requirements and should be a design complete in itself. The front panel is the most important. It must carry legibly and prominently the title and author's name and sometimes additional information in type or hand-lettered forms. The young illustrator learns to his consternation that the publisher usually regards these elements as more important than the pictorial or design embellishments.

The illustrator may or may not supply the hand-lettering or type specifications for these elements, but he must provide suitable space for them and should at least suggest the character of the letter forms. Suitable space means prominent space at least for the title, with the pictorial subject matter arranged about it. If the illustrator knows enough about type forms, he may indicate the type faces and sizes on a layout sketch, which can be set by a typographic service, and the proofs can be pasted in position on the picture. Most publishers warn their designers not to carry lettering too close to the edges — a margin of a half inch is a safe one.

The picture matter is usually best presented in a simple, bold, and arresting way, for it is the purpose of the jacket to attract the eye and coax the hand to pick up the book. In addition, the picture should create a climate or atmosphere that will arouse interest and convey something of the spirit of the book. Children's book jackets not only do this, they also tend to convey a message to the age group for which the book is suited.

Most jacket designs bleed at the top and bottom edges for trimming. At the right and left the flaps fold inside the covers. The flaps themselves usually carry advertising blurbs.

The shelfback panel presents its own design difficulties. Usually narrow, it tends to make the illustrator feel cramped. Although it must be considered as part of the whole design area, of which the front is the most important, the shelfback must be complete in itself, because when the book is lined up with others on the shelf it is the only part visible. It must carry a good deal of lettering: title, author's name, publisher's name and/or colophon, and sometimes the illustrator's name. The usual narrowness of the panel makes it difficult to squeeze all these lines of lettering across the width of the shelfback, and when the spine is

LEONA PIERCE
Woodcut jacket in three colors for
"Who Likes the Sun?"
Harcourt, Brace and Company

particularly narrow this is impossible. The only recourse is to run the lettering vertically instead of horizontally. In this case, the custom is to run the lettering so that it is right side up when the book is lying on its back. In England, the custom is the reverse.

Scant room is left for pictorial comment but sometimes a significant image of something discussed in the text can be centered between the title and author's name at the top, and the publisher's name at the bottom, which is the usual position for these elements.

The back, decorated more frequently on children's books than on those for adults, should contain a continuation of the themes on the face and backbone. When the jacket is flattened out it should be a homogeneous and consistent design, and at the same time the various panels should be complete in themselves. All in all, these are difficult demands to satisfy, and jacket design brings into play all the resources of the illustrator.

REMY CHARLIP
Jacket in two colors for
"A Day of Winter"
Alfred A. Knopf

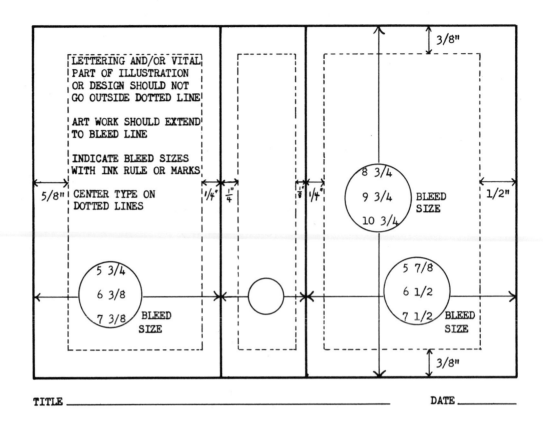

LETTERING AND/OR VITAL PART OF ILLUSTRATION OR DESIGN SHOULD NOT GO OUTSIDE DOTTED LINE

ART WORK SHOULD EXTEND TO BLEED LINE

INDICATE BLEED SIZES WITH INK RULE OR MARKS

CENTER TYPE ON DOTTED LINES

5/8"   1/4" 1/4"   1/8" 1/4"   3/8"   1/2"

8 3/4
9 3/4   BLEED
10 3/4   SIZE

5 3/4
6 3/8
7 3/8   BLEED
         SIZE

5 7/8
6 1/2
7 1/2   BLEED
         SIZE

3/8"

TITLE _____   DATE _____

THE CASING

Under the jacket is the stiff-sided casing. Often the illustrator has little to do with this. Sometimes he may choose the color and quality of the cloth that covers it, and may place the title, author's name, and publisher's name on the spine (often the same arrangement as that used on the jacket). Sometimes he may design an image to be used on the front. Some cover fabrics may be printed by an offset or silk-screen method, in which case the image may be rendered in black, white, or in color, just like any other illustration. Many covers are stamped under pressure by a brass die. If this is done, an ink drawing must be made for the die. It must be bold and simple, without delicate lines, because both the surface of the cloth and the pressure of the press that prints the design defeat delicacy. Any color can be die-stamped, including the metallic inks, gold, silver and aluminum. If no ink is used, the sunken image is called *blind* stamping.

140

THE END PAPERS

Inside the front cover and glued flatly to its back is half of a sheet of paper. The other half is not fastened down and acts as the first two pages of the book. Fastened to the inside of the back cover is a counterpart sheet. These are the *end papers.* Usually these sheets are blank white paper but sometimes they are colored, decorated, or used as a picture area. In this case the first end paper acts as a pictorial threshold to the book. It should say "Welcome." Usually, it is treated more decoratively than realistically and its pattern gives some pleasant hints of the general spirit of the book. It may be printed in two or more flat, muted colors, often upon a colored paper stock. In most cases, the design bleeds on all four trimmed sides. Sometimes an allover repetitive pattern is used, but when a pictorial composition is employed the artist must take care not to place a dominant form where it will be distorted by the center fold in the sheet.

Endpapers by ROGER DUVOISIN *for*
"Veronica"
Alfred A. Knopf

MARCIA BROWN
Half of endpapers for
"Once a Mouse"
Charles Scribner's Sons

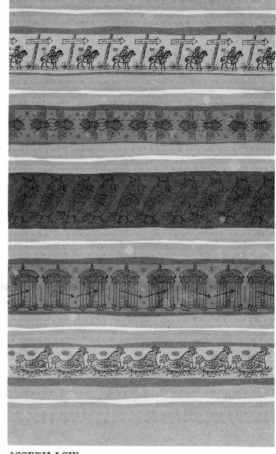

JOSEPH LOW
Half of endpapers for
"Mother Goose Riddle Rhymes"
Harcourt, Brace and Company

DAHLOV IPCAR
Endpapers for
"Deep Sea Farm"
Alfred A. Knopf

THE FRONT MATTER

Between the front and back end papers lie the bound signatures or core of the book. Almost always, before we come to the text proper, there are a number of pages that have special functions. These are the *front matter*. They can be abbreviated or extended, according to the character of the book, but usually have somewhat the following pattern: The first two pages may often be blank, with the third (right hand) containing a *half title*. This is nothing more than a preliminary title set in relatively modest type size and sometimes embellished by a small decorative spot drawing.

This half title is usually followed by a double page containing the frontispiece (left) and the title page (right). It is a traditional arrangement, with a pictorial composition on the frontispiece, and letter forms (usually type) and sometimes a spot drawing on the title side. Today, the frontispiece page is often left blank, or the double page becomes a joint title and frontispiece. In other words, the title page lettering is arranged to spread across both pages; pictorial elements likewise weave across the whole sheet and the double page becomes a unified design. This concept is popular now, because it allows more freedom for imaginative maneuver. The space is larger and more horizontal and the interplay of picture and letter forms offers endless combinations. As always when designing for a double page, the center fold must be reckoned with, and important design and letter forms kept away from its gutter.

The Sleeping　Beauty

From the Tales of CHARLES PERRAULT

Music by PETER ILYICH TSCHAIKOVSKY

Adapted and Illustrated by

WARREN CHAPPELL

New York: Alfred·A·Knopf

WARREN CHAPPELL
Doublepage title for
"The Sleeping Beauty"
Alfred A. Knopf

If the more traditional method of separate frontispiece and title page is accepted, there is still the obligation of balancing the two pages so that there is a feeling of joint unity. The composition used for the frontispiece is always considered to be of particular importance. One of the finest compositions among the illustrations should be used. It should deal with some dramatic episode, or typify the character of the text. Obviously, a knowledge of letter forms and type faces is essential in designing to meet these problems.

After the title page, a number of pages may intervene before the beginning of the text proper, depending upon the character and size of the book. The first such page contains the copyright information. There may or may not be a dedication page, and books must have a page or more for a preface and/or an introduction. A book of reasonable size often has a contents page, and sometimes there is a list of illustrations. Finally, another half title, and the body text is ready to begin. Any or all of these pages, with the exception of the copyright page, may be designed for spot decorations at the discretion of the illustrator.

ALDREN WATSON
Title page, "Fairy Tales of the Grimm Brothers"
Peter Pauper Press

MARCIA BROWN
Title page, "Once A Mouse"
Charles Scribner's Sons

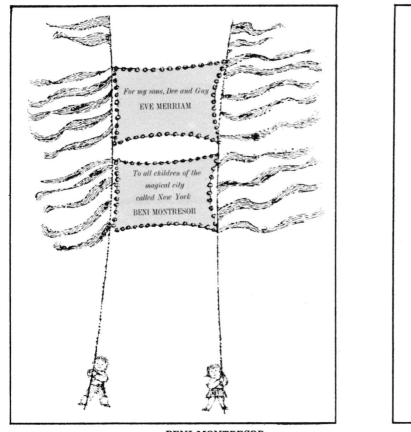

BENI MONTRESOR
An unusual dedication page from
"Mommies At Work."
Alfred A. Knopf

FEODOR ROJANKOVSKY
Half-title for
"The Whirly Bird"
Alfred A. Knopf

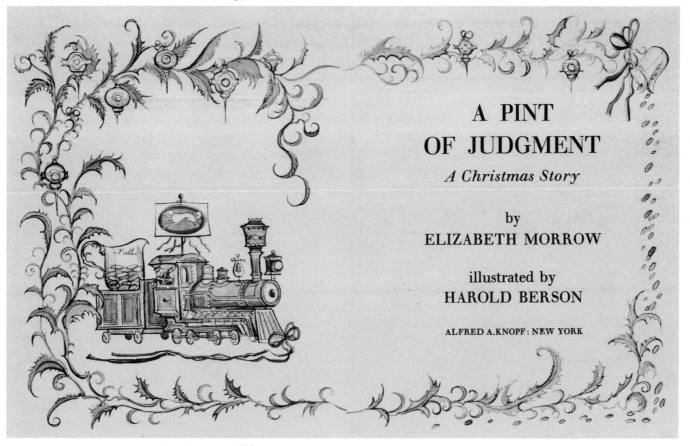

A PINT
OF JUDGMENT
A Christmas Story

by
ELIZABETH MORROW

illustrated by
HAROLD BERSON

ALFRED A. KNOPF : NEW YORK

HAROLD BERSON
Combined frontispiece and title page from
"A Pint of Judgment"
Alfred A. Knopf

THE BODY OF THE BOOK

The text proper may be richly or sparsely illustrated; but no matter what the number of pictures, they should be conceived as a group and not piecemeal. Not until the entire series is decided upon, the locations selected, and all of the illustrations are in sketch form, should individual pictures be begun and completed. There are many hazards in the way of unity and consistency in a series of pictures, and piecemeal completion only adds another.

The sketch stage may be short or long, depending upon the artist's ability, experience and other circumstances. Usually there is a groping stage, when sketch after sketch is discarded, but sketching should continue until clarity and satisfaction are reached. The sketching stage may well be interrupted by periods of research, particularly if the subject matter is unfamiliar. Many illustrators consider it the most important and most difficult part of the job. Most of the important decisions are made then. Once a satisfactory set of sketches has been assembled, the task is more than half over. For the experienced professional the final execution is relatively easy.

As soon as a series of pictures is contemplated, the problem of their distribution arises. Pictures cannot be dropped into a text haphazardly. The normal reader expects relatively even distribution. The artist prefers to picture only the incidents that excite him, but these seldom fall in an even progression. So the illustrator, dividing the number of pictures to be used into the number of text pages, arrives at the interval unit of pages between pictures. This interval does not have to be followed rigidly, only approximately; nonetheless, it limits the illustrator's choice of subject. He learns to be philosophical about the distribution.

The number of pictures and the general appearance of the book will be settled with the editor at the very start, but the illustrator is often given a good deal of latitude as to shapes, sizes, and general layout. Satisfactory distribution of pictures is expected from him as a matter of course. If he wishes his illustrations to have special characteristics, such as bleed edges or pictures running into the gutters and even across the double page, he must first have the sanction of the editor, because not all printing facilities permit these liberties. He will adhere rigidly to type page, all-over page, and any other dimensions that are given to him. Taking liberties with these can be costly and troublesome.

146

white bird sitting on a branch, which sang so charmingly that they could not help stopping to listen. When it had done, it flapped its wings and flew a short distance. Then it stopped and waited as if for them to catch up. They followed it and at last it led them to a small house, upon the roof of which it settled. They went up to the house and were astonished to find it was built of bread, with a roof made of cake and windows of barley sugar.

29

HENRY C. PITZ
Double page design for
"Hansel and Gretel"
Evergreen Books
Limited Editions Club

Although the shape of pages for picture books for the very young is often horizontal, most page proportions are vertical. This becomes a limiting factor for the illustrator, for many subjects seem to cry out for a horizontal treatment. There are, however, ways of providing a variety of shapes. The artist may elect to include many half-page pictures, which are usually wider than they are high. He may plan partial or complete double-page pictures. The partial double-page, using small amounts of text, can give him a wide variety, as is shown in some of the miniature layouts on this page. Very long, shallow picture shapes can be obtained by making strip panels across the double-page.

Small spot illustrations are another way of achieving variety. Theoretically, they can be any shape, but if they necessitate setting the text in short measure (less than the prevailing type-page width), the cost of composition goes up.

Today the squared-up picture, with rigid right-angled boundaries, is less popular than it was formerly. The vignette, or irregular shape without uniformly sharp edges is in greater use since it introduces a note of informality and permits the white of the paper to circulate through the picture.

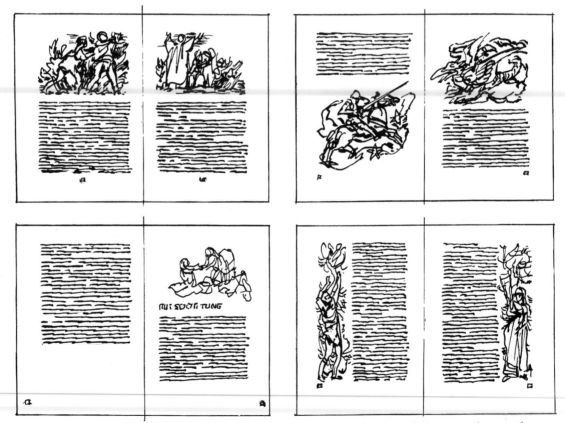

Small sketches offering several suggestions for double-page layouts involving pictorial and type elements.

THE SLEEP

FIFTEEN or sixteen years went by. The King and Queen were away at one of their country houses, and the little Princess, having nothing else to do, went roaming about the palace. She wandered from room to room, and from floor to floor, until she came to the top of one of the towers. There she found a tiny attic, where a kindly old woman was sitting and spinning. This old woman had never heard of the King's orders against using the distaff.

"What are you doing, good woman?" asked the Princess.

"Why, I'm spinning, my pretty dear," answered the woman, who did not know who her visitor was.

"It looks very interesting," said the Princess. "May I try to spin?"

WARREN CHAPPELL
Double page design for
"The Sleeping Beauty"
Alfred A. Knopf

1. New Folks Coming

ALL THE Hill was boiling with excitement. On every side there rose a continual chattering and squeaking, whispering and whistling, as the animals discussed the

[11]

ROBERT LAWSON
Chapter opening page for
"Rabbit Hill"
Viking Press

149

The chapter openings can be another important design item. The depth of the text on the open page of each chapter may be varied, open space at the top to be left free or filled with a pictorial spot, as the illustrator wills. Usually the chapter openings are uniform throughout the book, but there is no reason why they should not be varied, as long as there is a feeling of design consistency. Formerly, when a chapter text ended high on the page, a decoration for the space below, called a tail-piece, was popular. This is no longer so, but there is no reason why, on occasion, a decorative tail-piece should not be used. Our age, as all others, has created a definite design-climate; and it is only too easy to become dominated by it and lose one's sense of design independence.

It is very necessary to be aware of the design solutions of our time, to examine and study the current books and to understand the latest trends; but it is just as necessary not to become victimized by them. Present day design, lively and rewarding though it is, is not the last word. It will change. The change may be for better or for worse, but change of some sort is inevitable. The illustrator or designer who allows his design resources to stiffen completely in his early years will eventually move into a forlorn future.

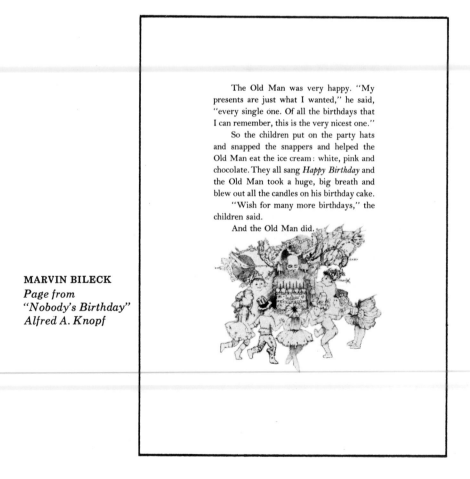

MARVIN BILECK
*Page from
"Nobody's Birthday"
Alfred A. Knopf*

150

R de a

Ban

CHAPTER 12

Typography and Book Design

JOSEPH LOW
Mother Goose Riddle Rhymes
Harcourt, Brace and Company

TYPE IS THE MOST IMPORTANT ELEMENT in most books. Even in the young child's picture books it is still a factor of great moment. No book could be considered well designed unless its type faces were well chosen, its size appropriate, and the type panels well proportioned and well printed. And the relation between type and illustration must be a successful one.

The illustrator or designer who lays out a book knows that its pictures can suffer greatly or be enhanced by the way surrounding type areas are handled. Illustrations are almost always near neighbors of type in some form, and they must be compatible.

Obviously, the designer or illustrator must know something about type, the characteristics of the more important type faces, the sizes, the leading, the way type is set up or composed and how it is printed. The world of type has a vocabulary of its own and the most important terms, at least, must be learned. Type has its own system of measurement too. Below are the absolutely essential terms.

Pica: One-sixth of an inch. The master unit of measurement.

Point: One seventy-second of an inch or one-twelfth of a pica. A necessary breakdown of the pica. Usually used to designate the size of a type face or the space between lines of type (leading).

Size: The size of the type to be used, always given in points (ten-point, twelve-point, etc.). This is not the distance from the top to bottom

151

of the letter itself but the full measurement of the metal base from which each letter projects.

Face: The design of type to be used. There are hundreds of type faces in use in the book field, although only a few dozen are in common use. Some are very similar, some very different. Some are adaptations of traditional faces used by the old printers, others are new creations.

Measure: The width of a line or word. Almost always given in picas.

Style, specifications, or *specs:* Complete instructions giving details for the setting of type for the complete book, as *size, face, measure, spacing,* or *leading, chapter heading, folio, number of pages, page length,* etc.

Leading: The distance in points between lines of type.

There are two necessary tools for every designer: a type ruler, which is scaled to picas and points, and a type book or books. Type books are usually very expensive but sometimes they can be obtained free from type founders, composition houses, or printers.

When type faces are studied, it is soon discovered that, although types are clearly marked by the point system (eight-point, ten-point, etc.), not all types of the same point size occupy the same amount of space. This is because, as was said above, the point size refers to the size of the metal block, or slug, upon which each letter is cast; the height, width, thickness, and character of individual letters can vary greatly from face to face. For this reason, in calculating spacing for a twelve-point face, to take an example, there is not a prevailing unit of twelve-point type that can be used. Each face is a law unto itself. This is where the type book is of great use to the artist designing a page. It will have sample lines of various faces in the more frequently used sizes. These lines must be measured to find the average number of letters and spaces that will appear in a line of given length.

Another factor that prevents exact measurement is that in any given type face many letters will be of different widths — an "i" is always narrower than a "w" for instance. The type designer works by the law of averages. Once he has estimated the number of *characters* (letters, spaces, and punctuation marks) in an average line, he uses that as a unit of measurement.

BASKERVILLE—12 POINT
How is one to assess and evaluate a type face in terms of its esthetic design?

BODONI BOOK—12 POINT
How is one to assess and evaluate a type face in terms of its esthetic design?

FUTURA MEDIUM—12 POINT
How is one to assess and evaluate a type face in terms of its esthetic design?

CALEDONIA—12 POINT
How is one to assess and evaluate a type face in terms of its esthetic de

CASLON OLDSTYLE—12 POINT
How is one to assess and evaluate a type face in terms of its esthetic de

GARAMOND—12 POINT
How is one to assess and evaluate a type face in terms of its esthetic design ? Ho

NEWS GOTHIC—12 POINT
How is one to assess and evaluate a type face in terms of its esthetic

PALATINO—12 POINT
How is one to assess and evaluate a type face in terms of its esthetic

TIMES ROMAN—12 POINT
How is one to assess and evaluate a type face in terms of its esthetic desi

WEISS ROMAN—12 POINT
How is one to assess and evaluate a type face in terms of its esthetic design ? How

Type specimens courtesy of Charles A. Benson, Inc. Advertising Typography, New York.

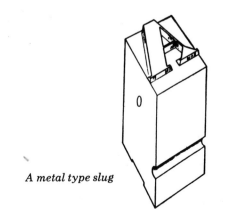

A metal type slug

The estimate of the total type space of a book proceeds by multiplication of *characters per line* by *lines per page*, which gives the number of characters per type page. This figure, divided into the number of characters in the manuscript, will show the number of type pages required in the book.

The above system of estimating can proceed by units of words instead of characters, but the character count is the more accurate. After the number of type pages has been ascertained, space allowances must be made for chapter headings, miscellaneous pages at the beginning of the book *(front matter),* and illustrations.

The number of pages in a book is important from a manufacturer's standpoint. Multiples of sixty-four pages are excellent, since many books are printed sixty-four pages at a time on one large sheet. Thirty-two, sixteen, eight, and four page units are good in diminishing order, except in special cases where small presses are involved.

For mechanical reasons, then, it is often necessary to make readjustments in some of the estimated factors: changes in type face, in width of lines, or depth of type page. These mechanical limitations can be irksome, but they must be obeyed before the designer is free to enjoy his aesthetic urges.

EDWARD BAWDEN
Tales of Troy and Greece
Faber and Faber

One little
Two little
Three little Indians,
Four little
Five little
Six little Indians,
Seven little
Eight little
Nine little Indians,
Ten little Indian boys.

J. P. MILLER
A Wonderful House
Golden Press

PAUL RAND
Sparkle and Spin
Harcourt, Brace and Company

A word is a thing
you heard or saw
or can even draw a
picture of.
Words are the names of objects
like book and doll and chair
or of animals
like bird and dog and bear.

...:!?;

AB
CD
EF
GH
IJ
KL
MN
OP
QR
ST
UV
WX
YZ

The weight and character of line in the illustrations also should have some relationship to the type face selected. Often the designer selects the type face to cooperate with the pictures, although sometimes the reverse is true. Occasionally, an illustrator is tempted to use an exotic type face because it goes well with his pictures; but here another factor enters: legibility. There are many spectacular and unusual type faces *(display types)*, which excite and delight the eye for a line or two but which bore and repulse if pursued page after page. The so-called *book types* have stood the test of countless hours of reading and have survived because they do not weary.

Whether the illustrator designs his own book or not, he has to realize that his illustration will appear in a setting and that that setting will be largely type. Picture and text are bound to influence each other, beneficially or adversely. Who would choose any but the way of cooperation between them?

f Reproduction

ATION IS AN ART OF REPRODUCTION. The drawing or painting that the artist considers finished may be ready to leave his hands, but it only represents a midway point in the journey to completion. There is a great deal to be done before it exists on the printed page and is in the hands of the ultimate reader. The picture will pass through many hands. It will pass from paper to photographic film to metal, and to paper again before it is truly an illustration.

Although a picture is out of the control of the artist and moves through a series of stages, with change, distortion, or even downright spoilage possible at every stage, the possibility of trouble can be minimized by an experienced illustrator. His pictures can be prepared so as to prevent difficulties for engraver and printer. The more the illustrator knows about reproduction, the better able he is to ensure good reproduction of his drawings. Also, the fact that this knowledge can often reduce engraving costs, is particularly pertinent to the novice illustrator, who is often given assignments in which economy is important.

Methods of reproduction have been part of the artist's craft for centuries, and for many years these methods were relatively simple and were practiced largely by the artists themselves. They were *direct* methods, largely hand methods. Three-quarters of a century ago when the invention of the photomechanical methods of the line cut and halftone plate was accompanied by rapid improvements in printing presses and techniques, the present day army of illustrative artists of all kinds was made possible. These new methods called for specialists of many types. The artist became one cog in the wheel of reproduction. These photomechanical processes are *indirect*.

All methods available to the artist may first be divided into *direct* and *indirect*, and each of these categories can be divided into three basic methods of reproducing and printing pictures.

DIRECT (largely hand)

I. *Relief or raised printing* woodcut, wood engraving, linoleum cut, and relief etching.

II. *Intaglio or below-surface printing* etching, dry point, copper or steel engraving, aquatint, mezzotint.

III. *Surface or planographic printing* lithographic, stencil, silk-screen.

INDIRECT (mechanical)

I. *Relief or letter press printing* line plate, halftone, and electro-plates made from them.

II. *Intaglio or below-surface printing* photogravure.

III. *Surface or planographic printing* lithograph, offset, collotype.

The three basic methods of reproduction, *relief, intaglio,* and *planographic,* may be defined very briefly: *relief* is *above* the surface printing; *intaglio* is *below* the surface printing, and *planographic* is *on* the surface printing.

RELIEF

Of the three processes, the relief method is the easiest one for most to understand and the one with which more people are likely to have some experience. Its earliest form was the woodcut, in use today by many of our print-making artists and popular in many high school classes, where linoleum is often substituted for wood. In practice, a design is drawn upon a block of either material, usually in black. When the black drawing is complete, the unblackened portions are cut down to a depth of perhaps one-eighth of an inch by chisels, gouges, and knives. This leaves the black drawing standing upon the surface of the block, with the other spaces lowered. The design is now in *relief*. An ink-charged roller passed over the block leaves ink on these high spots, and a sheet of paper laid upon the block and pressed down will have a print of the inked design transferred to it.

This is a *direct* type of relief printing. Almost all book illustration in relief is obtained, however, by the photomechanical or *indirect* method. The photomechanical counterpart of the woodcut is the *line cut.*

Briefly, this is how *line cuts* — also known as *engravings* or plates — are made. The artist's picture is placed before a camera, adjustments are made to reduce it to proper reproduction size, and a photograph of it is made on a glass plate. The plate is developed and the film is hardened, stripped from its glass foundation and transferred to a sensitized metal plate. This plate is usually zinc, sometimes copper. Exposed to light, the image is now transferred onto the metal plate. The plate is developed and washed. The metal plate now contains a tracery of film that follows the black lines of the drawing. The other portions of the plate are clear. The metal plate is next placed in a bath of acid, and the unprotected portions of the plate are eaten into, or "bitten" by the acid. When sufficiently bitten, the plate is nailed to a wooden block, type-high, and is ready to make its journey through the press.

At this point the line cut, if examined, will appear pitted with valleys or depressions in the metal. These valleys will not receive ink and will leave white paper in the reproduction. The upper surface of the metal will repeat in reverse the tracery of black lines in the drawing. These upper or relief surfaces will receive ink and print the image of the original picture.

Diagram of a line plate
showing raised design as it leaves the imprint
upon the paper

159

In this brief description, only the essentials have been discussed. A good deal of detail and some of the minor operations have been omitted, for the artist need not necessarily be acquainted with all the intricacies. The fundamental operations must be comprehended. Since complete understanding is likely to come only by actually observing the process, one or more visits to photoengraving houses should be part of the illustrator's education.

The similarity of the line cut to the wood or linoleum block will be seen. It is an excellent method of reproduction, and at its best can deliver a facsimile of the artist's work. Because the material is metal, fine lines can be obtained. But the line cut has severe limitations. It can only reproduce copy made up of black lines or shapes as the tonal grays are beyond its powers.

The reproduction of tonal gray is made by the companion invention of the line cut, the *halftone*. The method of making a halftone is very much the same, the chief difference being the intervention of a glass halftone screen when photoengraving the copy.

This glass screen has two series of parallel lines placed at right angles to each other. When this lined screen is placed in the camera before the film, it breaks up the pictorial copy into hundreds of tiny dots. These dots, looked at under a magnifying glass, are larger and closer together where the copy is dark, and smaller and farther apart where the copy is light.

By making the lines of the screen closer or farther apart, the dots can be made very fine or coarse. The lines on the screen vary from forty-five to eighty to the inch for coarse screens (used principally for the newspaper work), to very fine screens of two hundred lines to the inch that can be printed successfully only on coated papers. In between are the one hundred and twenty and one hundred and thirty-three fine screens used for most work.

After photographing the picture through the screen, the process is much the same as that followed in the line cut. The negative is transferred to a copper plate, and after treatment is etched with acid. The etching needs to be more expert than in the case of the line cut. It must be done by stages, and from time to time the lighter parts must be stopped out with acid resist so that the deeper parts can be re-etched.

This is a mechanical process, but nevertheless a good deal of skilled handwork is necessary if the final illustration is to retain the same balance of values as are in the original copy. In this etching stage, or series of stages, certain refinements can be introduced, such as deep etching (which removes all the small dots in the highlights and white spaces and allows them to print clear and sparkling).

The completely etched halftone is tacked onto a type-high wooden block and is ready for the printer. The finished halftone usually requires a magnifying glass to discover the multitude of tiny dots that crowd the surface of the metal. These dots are like the tops of tiny mountain peaks surrounded by valleys of etched metal. The peaks are all on the same level (the original level of the bare sheet of metal), and they are now ready to receive ink from the rollers and transfer their inked image onto the paper.

At the left is an 80 screen halftone (80 dots to the inch) of a photograph. The right hand halftone is an enlargement of a small portion of the same photograph which reveals the dot pattern.

161

INTAGLIO

Intaglio is the name given to all the methods by which a print is taken from the recesses of an incised surface. It includes line engraving, mezzotint, etching, dry point, aquatint and photoengraving. Photoengraving is an indirect method of reproduction; all the rest are direct.

The illustrator is concerned only with the indirect method, photogravure. This is the method that prints many of our mass magazines, Sunday supplements and some of our books. Printing from copper cylinders makes it possible to turn out editions rapidly.

In preparing the copper cylinder, the image is printed on its curved surface photographically. A ruled screen of lines at right angles is placed over the image. This screen is protected by acid resist and when the cylinder is etched the image is composed of a multitude of tiny pits, which, because of the superimposed ruled screen, are arranged in a uniform grid pattern. Under the magnifying glass this grid of tiny pits is seen to be shallow for the lights and deep for the darks.

For printing, the cylinder is inserted in the press and coated with a special thin ink that fills all the tiny pits or cells. The surplus ink is scraped from the cylinder surface by a scraper blade and when the cylinder rotates against the paper, the sheet, being somewhat absorbent, draws up more ink from the deeper cells to form the darks, and lesser amounts from the shallow cells to make the lighter tints. The photogravure cells produce dots of even size, but the varying amounts of ink absorbed from these cells produces a wide range of grays from the lightest to the darkest. In this method, the printed image comes from ink held in cells sunken below the surface of the metal. This is in contrast to the relief method, where the image comes from inked metal standing up from the plate.

Photogravure at its best produces a fine velvety impression. It tends to soften edges and contrasts and to blend tones, which is often very desirable for pictorial material. Type, however, is given a slightly foggy look by photogravure, and so it is usually used for large editions of the picture book variety.

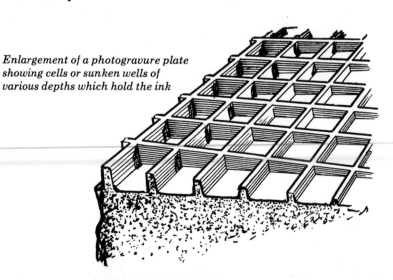

Enlargement of a photogravure plate showing cells or sunken wells of various depths which hold the ink

162

PLANOGRAPHIC

Planographic printing includes lithography and collotype; but the second, while it is a beautiful method, is very special, expensive, and not used very often. The illustrator is not likely to encounter it.

Lithography was discovered in 1796, when Aloys Senefelder (1771-1834) discovered that by drawing on a slab of local limestone with a greasy crayon, then wetting and inking the stone, the water would repel the ink except where the water itself had been repelled by the greasy tracery of the crayon drawing. The inked image could be transferred to paper by pressure. This was a direct method which artist print-makers still use today with little variation in practice since Senefelder's time.

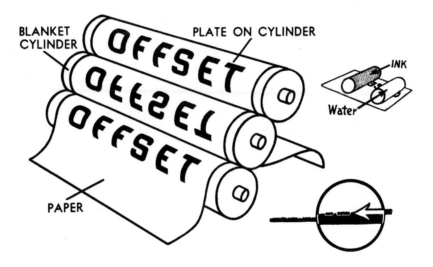

Planographic printing is based on the principle that water and grease do not mix. The image on the surface is a grease substance. Water is applied to the plate surface and is repelled by the greasy areas. Then ink is applied and adheres only to the greasy image area. The plate does not print directly on the paper but transfers the image to a rubber (blanket) cylinder which then offsets the ink to the paper.

For commercial use, lithography has joined with photography and high speed presses to produce the indirect method of photolithography or photolitho-offset. The lithographic stone, heavy and cumbersome, has been replaced by large sheets of thin, flexible zinc. These can be wrapped around press cylinders for rapid printing. These zinc sheets are coated with a sensitive emulsion on which the images are printed photographically, much in the same way that halftones are produced. In lithography, the areas around the dots are not etched into the metal, leaving the dots in relief. The dots are simply etched clear of grease. This leaves the zinc sheet covered with halftone dots *on the emulsion,* neither above nor below the metal surface. All of these dots are greasy and will *accept* ink. They are surrounded by tiny areas of bare metal which, when covered with water, will *repel* ink. When an ink roller passes over this wetted surface it leaves ink on the emulsion (grease) dots; the clear wet portions of the metal will not accept the ink. When brought into pressure contact with paper the ink dots transfer the image to it. This is called direct lithography, but today most lithographic printing is by *offset* or *photolitho-offset.* This means that in the process of printing, an additional roller has been interposed. The sequence is now this: the ink roller transfers ink to the zinc roller containing the image; the zinc roller in turn moves in contact with a rubber (offset) roller transferring the image to it; and finally the offset roller moves against the paper sheet, printing it with the image.

Recently, the method has expanded greatly, partly at the expense of the letterpress (relief) methods. Its use in the book field seems to be increasing. The offset impression is soft and blended. Sometimes it grays the impression of type, but it is excellent in picking up the subtle nuances of a pencil line or brush stroke.

JEROME SNYDER
One Day in Ancient Rome
Harcourt, Brace and Company

CHAPTER **14**

Preparing Pictures for Reproduction

AN UNDERSTANDING OF THE FUNDAMENTAL PROCESSES of reproduction is the basis for numerous concrete practices that are the day by day stock in trade of the professional illustrator. These practices must be consciously applied at first. They may seem burdensome, but eventually they become almost automatic. Illustrators of all kinds require reproduction know-how to solve many of their problems, but the book illustrator requires more than most. Book publishers wage constant battles against production costs and often expect the artist to adopt methods that are more economical but entail greater effort for him, such as making careful and laborious color separations. The most important of these procedures and facets of reproduction are described below:

BLEEDS

Two terms that are frequently encountered by the book illustrator are *bleed* and *bleeds* used both as nouns and verbs. To bleed means to run an illustration to the trimmed edge or edges of a page. Actually, such an illustration is printed larger than the size of the trimmed page, and in the binding operations the cutting machines sheer off the excess picture. The excess trimmed sliver of paper is a *bleed*.

Why bother to print excess picture when it will be trimmed off as waste? Because the mechanics of printing make exact register and positioning difficult. For one thing, sheets of paper are very susceptible to stretching and contraction due to humidity changes. Besides, as they speed through the rapid presses, slight alterations take place, with the result that from time to time telltale slivers of white paper would appear on some of the margins if attempts were made to print a plate exactly to the edge. This is avoided by over-printing the edge and trimming the picture cleanly.

For the illustrator to make provisions for bleeds in his drawings is a very simple matter. He merely adds a thin strip of additional picture on those edges of his illustration that are to bleed. Editors often note the dimensions of the bleeds; if none is given, however, one-eighth of an inch is a fairly standard allowance. This, of course, is the reproduction size — if the picture is larger, and it usually is, the bleed sliver must be enlarged accordingly. Since this sliver is waste, nothing of pictorial importance should be put on it. In fact, the space is too narrow for anything except the basic tones or colors of the picture.

SIZES IN REPRODUCTION

Illustrations begin with a size. Usually the editor furnishes the illustrator with a set of dimensions, or if the illustrator is laying out the book himself, he will arrive at the dimensions. Once these dimensions have been decided, there is no *nearly* or *maybe* about it; they are precise and the artist is expected to heed them scrupulously.

This drawing by **LEO POLITI** *for "The Butterflies Come," Charles Scribner's Son, bleeds at the left and bottom of page*

If the artist were to make his pictures the same size as the reproduction dimensions, the matter would be very simple. But this seldom happens. Few artists like to work in the cramped space of the average book illustration. Moreover, most drawings are improved in sharpness by a reasonable degree of reduction. So most illustrations are drawn larger than the actual reproduction size.

The amount of enlargement varies with the individual artist. Occasionally, the degree of enlargement is dictated by the editor. The usual enlargements run from one and one-half times to three times reproduction size. The artist can choose his own size, but it must be in the same proportions as the reproduction size.

Laying out the enlarged size for an illustration is very simple in most cases. If the enlargement size is in an obvious ratio, as one and one-half or two times larger, it is an easy matter to multiply the reproduction dimensions by the enlargement factor. Sometimes, however, a more difficult degree of enlargement is desired, in which case some elementary geometry must be used. On the drawing paper, with T-square and angle, a base line for the drawing and one side at right angles should be laid out. Using these two lines from the corner thus established, lay out a rectangle the exact size of the reproduction desired. Through the diagonal corners of this rectangle draw a long diagonal extending out into the paper. From any desired point of this diagonal, a horizontal and vertical may be drawn to the two original lines, completing the larger rectangle. The larger rectangle will be in exact proportions to the smaller. The diagram on this page illustrates this method.

This geometrical method applies not only to rectangular forms but to more complex ones. Most irregular vignette shapes can be bounded by one or a series of rectangles or squares. Once in a while it may be necessary to introduce the triangle or circle.

The ability to gauge how well a certain reduction of one's drawing will reproduce comes from experience, but there is always the helpful rule that the looser and more open a drawing, the more reduction

Diagram illustrating the use of the diagonal drawn through any rectangle in order to obtain larger or smaller rectangles according to the same proportion.

it will stand without clogging. Every opportunity for comparing original art work with its reproduction should be seized upon.

Mechanically, it is just as easy to take small illustrative material and enlarge it to reproduction size as to do the reverse. Sometimes this is done, and sometimes copy is reproduced exact size. It depends upon the effect desired. But experience has shown that reduction of copy for reproduction gives the best results in the great majority of cases.

At right a drawing reproduced original size, above the same drawing reduced one-third, at left the drawing reduced two-thirds.

DRAWING FOR THE LINE CUT

A great deal of children's book illustration is reproduced by line cut, because it is much more economical than the halftone. It is also simpler and more certain. At best, it has a crispness and a brilliance that delights the eye and, in addition, it unites perfectly with type.

Line reproduction requires copy in which all the drawing is black on a white surface. Grays are achieved by the optical mixture of varying amounts of black lines or marks and white spaces. This means that the artist's paper is white and clean, that the pen strokes and brush or crayon marks are clear black, and that all pencil indications are cleaned from the finished drawing by gentle erasure.

Paper is important. It influences the character of a drawing. Smooth (hot-pressed) papers or illustrations boards are excellent for mechanical, slick, meticulous work; rough (cold-pressed) paper has some of the qualities of each, giving a slightly irregular line that has character, vigor and yet is susceptible to delicacy and grace. The artist should experiment with many kinds of paper, seeking for those which best convey his intentions and style.

A good quality paper is also important when corrections have to be made. Offending areas can be scraped out gently with a razor blade or whited out with poster or casein white. Major corrections often have to be made by pasting clean paper over the bungled part and redrawing. The patch should be pasted carefully, without blisters or curled edges, and the edges must show a continuation of the drawing lest a white line show up in the reproduction.

Paper is also important in the reproduced picture. For line work a smooth, good quality paper will give a clean, sharp impression, whereas a poor quality, blotter-like stock will give coarse and ragged impressions from the same plate. If the artist knows in advance the kind of paper on which his pictures will be printed, he can do a great deal to minimize the effects of inferior paper and poor printing.

To offset the effects of poor quality paper and/or inferior printing, the artist's drawing should be handled in a simple, bold way, the lines positive and weighty and any cross-hatching and textural manipulations held to a minimum. Fine lines and delicate tracery can be used when better paper and printing are available.

Many of today's children's books use two, three, or more colors printed from line plates. Although this method has its limitations, it is

ROBERT FAWCETT
A strong rendering in ink
excellent for good line reproduction
Young Hickory
Rinehart

capable of yielding beautiful and exciting work. It is popular also because it is much more economical than the *full-color* halftone method of using a set of four halftone plates; yellow, red, blue and black.

Art work for line color reproduction has to be prepared in a special way. Various methods are used but they all involve the making of *separations,* i.e. separate drawings for each color used. Sometimes a very simple method can be used; at other times it can be intricate, depending upon the effect that is desired. The drawing or drawings for such a picture in flat color have to be prepared in a certain way.

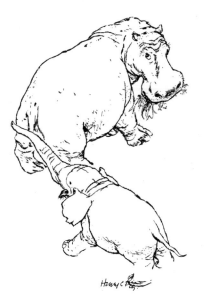

Three plates showing the development of two-color reproduction. Above, first, the master drawing reproduced in black, — next, the second color drawing reproduced in gray. Both drawings were executed in black ink and crayon. At left, the two combined to make the finished picture.

171

COLOR SEPARATIONS
FOR LINE REPRODUCTION

First, let us mention a method that will work for any problem in flat color reproduction; namely the making of a *separate* drawing for *each* color. Each drawing is made in *black* ink, no matter what color it is to be printed in later. First, a key drawing is made. The key drawing is the one that contains the plotting of the dominant color in the combination. This will often be printed in black. It usually contains the major forms in the composition.

When this is completed, register marks, or carefully drawn crosses are placed at the top and bottom. These are guides to insure perfect register, or an exact fit between the various drawings. Over the key drawing a sheet of acetate is fastened tightly and the register marks traced carefully. Then, using the key drawing as a guide, the parts of the picture that are to be printed in the second color are carefully drawn in black ink. If there is to be a third or fourth color, the procedure is repeated for each. If a color sample is provided for each color to be used, the drawings are now ready for the engraver. He will make a separate plate for each drawing and the register marks will enable the plates to be made in perfect relationships to one another. The printer will mix his inks to match the samples.

Drawing with transparent acetate overlay folded back. Ink has been drawn and traced on the overlay to indicate which portions of the design should be printed in the second color.

172

Although this is a simple method to understand, it is not always the most direct one. The principle of a separate drawing for each color remains (the student should keep that firmly fixed in his mind), but there are a number of ways of achieving it. There is one variation which you may adopt only if the two different color areas in your picture *do not* touch each other—in other words, the colors must be separated at least by a tiny sliver of white paper. In this method, draw in the key color in black ink, just as if you were making a pen drawing. Then draw in the design and areas of the second color (no matter what that second color may be) in red. You are using red because it is a color that will photograph as easily and darkly as black. Use a dark opaque red and avoid pinks. Your drawing is now ready for the engraver. You also need color swatches to show him the color of ink or inks to be used. While your drawing is in black and red, it can be printed in any two colors you or the art editor may order. The engraver is going to make two line cuts from your single picture, and the black and red not only will photograph easily, but will tell him just which areas go on each plate.

The next method can be used in those types of illustrations in which the black picture encloses the areas of the second color. Here we cannot use red because it would touch or pass through the black drawing and confusion would result—for remember that the camera does not discriminate between black and red. So we make use of the opposite photographic principle, remembering that pale blue makes no impression on the ordinary photographic plate.

The black drawing is made in the usual way, then, within the boundaries of black lines, wash in with pale, diluted blue watercolor those areas intended to be filled with the second color. A pale blue crayon may be used instead. If any area to be filled in with blue is not completely bounded by a black line or mass, one must be drawn in red. The engraver will know that it is temporary—just to give him a definite edge—and he will see that it does not appear in the finished plate. Again, one must realize that, although the drawing is in black and pale blue this time, it may be printed finally in any two colors. Of course, black is usually one of the colors, because that is ordinarily the color in which the type is printed.

If all the second color areas in a drawing are bounded by black lines or forms, we may choose to indicate the second color spotting on

173

an overlay, or sheet of tracing paper fastened over the black drawing. In this case, of course, the indications need not be made in pale blue; they may be made in the color in which the plate is to be printed.

There is another variation that has come into wider use recently: that involving the use of "blue proofs" or "blue bristols." In this method, the key drawing is prepared in the usual way and sent to the engraver. He will make a plate of it and send you several proofs printed in pale blue ink. Now you have before you a faint but complete image of your drawing in the actual size it will be reproduced. Upon this you draw, with black ink, the scheme for your second color. If the pale blue ink is somewhat greasy, as sometimes happens, and repels the ink, ox gall will make the surface workable as will saliva. Talcum powder can be helpful, too. This last mentioned method is excellent, particularly when the finished picture is to be in three, four, or more colors. It has, however, some drawbacks. One has to work small, in the same size as the reproduction, except for the first key drawing. Also the pale blue image is hard to see. Finally, if your drawings are needed in a hurry, this method may take too long, what with sending your drawing to the engraver and waiting for the blue proofs. Never embark on this method on your own initiative. You must consult with your editor so that he may make arrangements with the engraver.

The other methods can be used for more than two colors also, in fact, in certain cases, all three methods may be indicated in one set of drawings. Remember, the choice of methods depends largely on the effect desired. If you are ever in doubt about how to solve a problem in multiple color for line reproduction, you can always do it by making a *separate* drawing for each color, all of them in perfect register. It may not be the easiest or most straightforward way, but it will always work.

Another way of making separations by overlays is to utilize the light-box or even a large plate-glass window. To work this method, the master drawing must be on a lightweight paper, translucent enough for a strong source of light to shine through. Bond papers and good drawing stock of about seventy-two pound weight are usually excellent for both master drawing and overlays.

A light-box is a simple affair of a box with a glass top and a strong light bulb below. The master drawing is taped down on the glass top (or the window glass) and suitable register marks are ruled in.

Next a fresh sheet of translucent paper is taped over the master, the register marks are carefully traced on the new sheet, and then the lines and masses for the second color are drawn in with black ink. The master drawing showing through acts as an exact guide. The light-box method is accurate, relatively easy and permits the use of papers of different textures for each separation, if desired.

Another overlay method that has come into increasing use of late years involves the use of Bourges sheets. These are sheets of coated acetate, furnished in a wide variety of colors. When only one separation for a second color is needed, the red-orange sheet is used, but when more colors are necessary, and it is possible to choose them from the wide variety that Bourges offers, the final result of all overprintings can be seen if each separation is placed one upon another in accurate register.

These Bourges sheets are coated with a solid but transparent color, which means that the artist must remove the coating from the unwanted areas with a wooden stylus. The scratching effect of the stylus can be used to simulate a woodcut or wood engraving technique.

Diagram of a light-box showing strong source of light, glass surface for the papers, the key drawing taped on the glass and the paper for the overlay about to be placed over the key drawing.

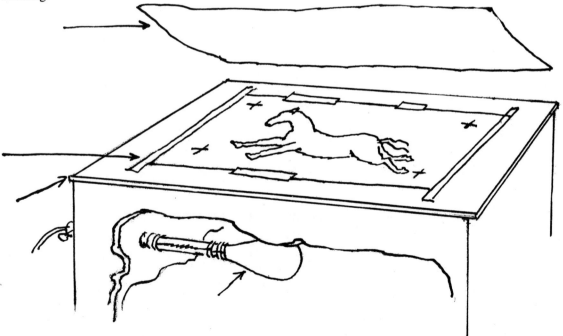

HALFTONE EFFECTS IN LINE

We have become acquainted with some of the limitations of line. Since the invention of halftone, efforts were made to simulate some of the modeling effects; the Ben-Day system of tints was perfected and has been used for many years. Lately, the use of transparent tinting films has somewhat superseded the Ben-Day screens, which have to be applied by the engraver. The use of lithographic pencil on grained paper (which can be reproduced in line), has also been used for many years.

The first column contains sample tints of Zip-a-tone, the second of Craftint. These are transparent films which can be cut to any shape and fastened to suitable areas of a drawing, as in the example on the opposite page. The third column contains sample tints of BenDay, which are indicated on a drawing by their numbers and are added to the finished plate by the engraver.

This last method, called the *Direct Contact* process, has been improved so that within the past few years it has become possible to produce multicolor work that has halftone properties by a series of line plates. This method is halfway between line and halftone. It escapes the high cost of four-color halftone and actually produces a livelier effect than most halftone, for it avoids the blurring of contrasts that normally mars the halftone.

The artist must make his own separation for this method, too. This is what is required of him. He should make the master drawing *reproduction size* on a transparent surface — sand-blasted acetate, grained vinylite and certain tracing papers that have a proper tooth. He can work with inked brush and pen, but the resources of the method reveal themselves when lithographic crayon or carbon black pencils, which have a wax binder, are used. The drawing made with these pencils on a properly grained surface will reveal itself under the magnifying glass as a collection of thousands of tiny specks of black, deposited on the crests of the irregular grains and surrounded by tiny threads or spaces of white, which are the valleys between the crests. A heavy stroke will fill most or all the valleys; a light stroke will only leave a few small specks on the surface.

Line drawing with the addition of various shading tints.

Grained tones produced by pencil crayon on textured surface board.

Since this drawing is actually a collection of numerous but tiny black marks, it will make suitable copy for a line reproduction. This *direct contact* method is only suitable for lithographic reproduction and printing. The artist's drawing is not placed before a camera but is locked in a vacuum frame in direct contact with a film; hence, its name. Theoretically, and often enough actually, this will produce a negative which will record every minute element of every stroke with complete fidelity, and then transfer all this to the printing plate and finally to the paper itself.

COLOR

The artist, after completing his reproduction size master drawing, must supply it with register marks and then successively fasten over it the red, yellow and blue separations. This is where experience counts. It is very difficult for the inexperienced to make a black mark on a separation and realize that it will be a light but vivid yellow. It is even more difficult to visualize what color will result from three overlapping areas drawn in black pencil on three separate sheets.

One help is to have samples of the three process colors before you and realize that a black mark is equal to the full intensity of any particular color. An artist's eye should be able to evaluate an area of tiny specks as a middle gray, for example, and then realize that on the blue plate it would be half the strength of the sample.

Since we can expect an artist to be versed in color theory, he should know what strength of tone on the yellow and red separations will produce a given orange and how much pencil work on the blue and yellow separations will produce a desired green. But the allover color scheme is not easy to visualize, even for the experienced artist. One helpful practice is to make the master (black) separation complete and rich in tonality. Then, if some mistakes have been made in primary color separations, they will probably be absorbed into the grays of the black plate.

This method, with its variations, is quite new. Changes and improvements can be looked for. In fact, the whole world of reproduction is far from static. The artist will never be able to rest on his oars with complete knowledge. There is always something new to be learned.

DRAWING FOR HALFTONE

Fewer technicalities are encountered in preparing pictorial copy for halftone reproduction than for the line cut, at least when color is involved. In the case of *full* or four-color reproduction the picture is painted with a full palette the way the artist hopes it will appear when printed. The basic colors involved — the primary colors, red, yellow, and blue, plus black to give depth and volume — are separated mechanically by successive camera shots through color-filter lens. The burden of making separations is no longer necessary.

Versatile as the four color process is, it also has its limitations. It reproduces some paintings faithfully, while it finds others difficult and is unable to render an accurate facsimile of color and tonal relationships. One commanding reason for this is that the process must work with a very limited palette. Over the years, it has hit upon three versions of the primary colors that yield the best all-round results for the majority of its problems. These so-called process colors — an acid yellow, an irritating red, and a rather pleasant blue, together with black — do achieve remarkable results, all things considered; but they cannot be expected to solve all problems equally well.

It is true that the primary colors can be mixed specially for a given job, but this is more expensive, and it seldom happens that a single picture is printed at one time in the publishing world. It is only economical to print a whole book series or an entire magazine at one time, and a special palette for one picture could be disastrous for others.

The illustrator gets the best results by working with the established process colors. He knows the look of them and tries to avoid extremely vivid hues. It always helps to base his pictures on a strong *tonal* scheme. The black and white values will be held by the black plate and will give body to the reproduction even if the primary color plates are not completely faithful.

It is important to remember that there is only one kind of red, yellow, and blue ink available at one time. That means for instance, that it is not possible to obtain an equally bright cerulean blue and violet-blue at the same time. If a blue with a little green in it is used, the cerulean will be excellent and the violet grayed. The two other primary colors work under the same disadvantage.

For all halftone work, color or monochrome, it is helpful to paint with greater contrasts than one expects in the reproduction and to define important edges of forms more sharply than usual. Doing this will tend to counteract the general softening effect of the process. The halftone screen robs a picture of its extremes of contrast. The dots gray down both the lights and the blacks. The screen also tends to blur edges slightly, so these effects must be compensated for in the artist's drawing.

N. M. BODECKER
Sylvester
Golden Press

ADRIENNE SEGUR
Thumbelina, Fun and Fancy
Golden Press

ERIK BLEGVAD
Where's Willie
Golden Press

The three process (primary) colors used in color printing. The overlaps of these three show the secondary colors produced. Usually a black plate is added to the primaries in order to give body and tonal strength to the picture.

RUDOLF FREUND
American Butterflies and Moths
Random House

W. W. DENSLOW
The Wonderful Wizard of Oz
Dover Publications

PART III. PROFESSIONAL PRACTICE

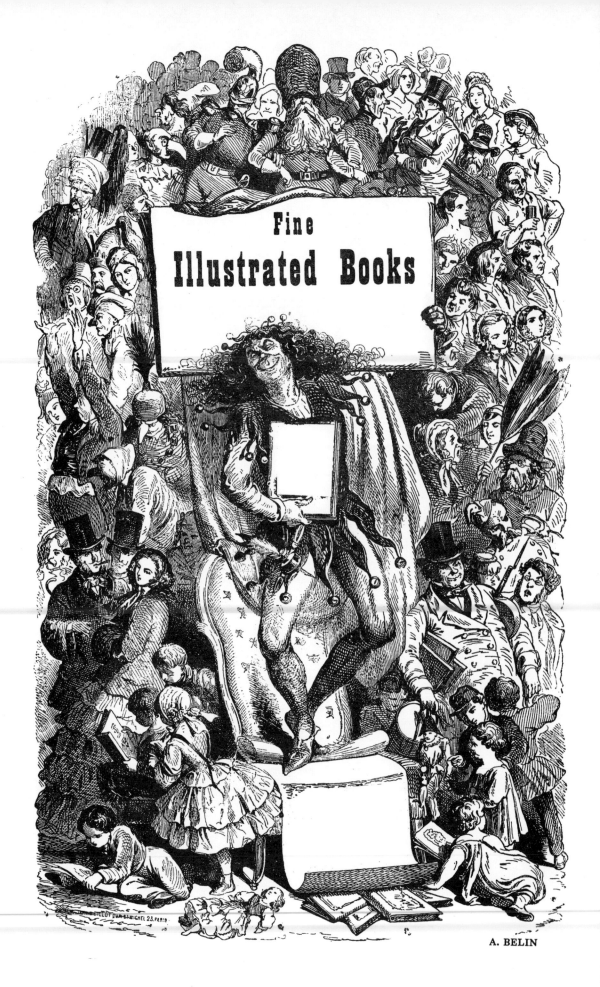

Fine
Illustrated Books

A. BELIN

GERALD ROSE
Old Winkle and the Seagulls
Faber and Faber

CHAPTER 15

Handling An Assignment

ILLUSTRATORS TEND TO BE INDIVIDUALISTS, and neither in their finished pictures nor in the stages that lead to completion do they conform to a set pattern. And yet, fully aware of their thousand-and-one personal idiosyncrasies, they do have their methods and procedures and, in a general way, they move from conception to the finished book in pretty much the same ways. There are certain procedures that are inevitable and which they share in common. The novice illustrator has not had the time or experience to work out an individual system but he can benefit from some basic suggestions.

An illustration assignment begins with a letter or telephone call from an editor. The illustrator has been picked, presumably because he or she is not only competent, but because the subject matter is congenial, because he or she is at home in the age group that is indicated, and because of general dependability. The text is summarized, the number and style of pictures indicated, the delivery date stated, and usually the fee set.

If the assignment is accepted, a text will be sent on. This may be in typewritten manuscript form or it may be set in type and appear in the shape of galley proofs — long, snaky strips of paper on which the text is printed in columns.

Every illustrator grinds his teeth at the inevitable and repetitive question, "Do you read the stories you illustrate?" The answer is, "Yes."

187

Probably the first time the manuscript is read quickly for information and flavor but then is followed by a more careful reading in order to find the most likely spots to be illustrated. These are marked on the margin, sometimes with little notes. If the text is at all fruitful in a picture-making sense, at the end of this reading there should be more picture possibilities than space provided for them. A third scanning should produce some order of distribution and some elimination by the artist of superfluous situations.

The incidents selected are now ready for sketch clarification. Most illustrators make their first sketches of the thumbnail variety, small and rapidly executed. Their purpose is to quickly explore and bring some clarification into the inviting images that up to then have only existed in the mind's eye. Each selected situation may require several of these quick sketches. Sometimes a situation is tantalizing in the number of solutions it suggests and elimination is difficult; other situations seem to call for one answer. It is general practice to carry the whole series of compositions through the thumbnail stage before moving on to more detailed work, for it enables the artist to visualize the whole set of potential pictures and to decide such things as whether the sketches of the series are too similar, too inconsistent, or if some important aspect of the text has been ignored.

The next stage is the larger sketch, usually the same size as the finished illustration. It may be drawn on tracing paper first, because changes and revisions can be made easily. By slipping one version under a clean sheet, you can trace off the wanted parts and add the new forms; when the revisions have reached the point of satisfaction, the composition may be readily traced on the final drawing paper or board for the finished rendering. During this stage, it may be necessary to refer back to the text from time to time to clarify details and facts.

At this point, when the full-size sketches are marshaled and approved, it might be well to pause and point out that the character and purpose of the intended book have a great deal to do with the procedures. If the book should be the picture-book type destined for very young children, almost certainly the artist has to construct a *dummy* showing the placement of pictures and type. If the book is of the teenage type and all the pictures are planned to be full pages, there is no need to prepare a *dummy*.

A *dummy* is a sketch facsimile of the book to come. It is the same

The stages of an illustration. First, small, quick sketches to crystallize a pictorial idea, then a drawing working out the forms and details from which the finished picture is traced.

HENRY C. PITZ
20,000 Leagues Under the Sea
Junior Deluxe Editions
Nelson Doubleday, Inc.

size, of course, with each page laid out the way it will appear in the finished volume. The type lines will be indicated by ruled lines or, if the text has been set and printed in galley form, by pasting the relevant amount of text in its proper place. The pictures are indicated in sketch form in their proper areas. Sometimes dummies are finished with a great deal of care and precision, especially when illustrators and authors are trying to sell a new picture-book idea to a publisher or when the dummy is to be used as an exact guide for the printer. At other times they may be very sketchy and abbreviated, when it is only necessary to project the general idea.

HENRY C. PITZ
*Dummy drawing of double-page endpapers
for book of fairy tales*

Dummies can be made up by cutting suitable paper to the proper size, folding and forming signatures. The signatures may be sewn or stapled at the folded edge. Publishers usually will provide the illustrator with his dummy, having them made up by a printer or paper house.

In the picture book for the young, the text is very short and should be set in large size, fourteen point or more, with a picture usually appearing on every page. Very little text will be on each page, sometimes only a line or two, but the type space should be accurately drawn or pasted in. The picture fits above, below or around the text. With color or halftone pictorial material, the text may be imprinted over part of the picture, provided this portion of the picture is light in tone and does not contain active or important forms. The text should never be illegible for young eyes.

With the completion of the dummy, the illustrator has an accurate idea of how the finished book will look. It will show how the pictures will look in relation to each other and the general impression the book will make as one turns the page. It will also furnish accurate sizes for each picture, no matter how oddly shaped they may be. Undoubtedly, the editor will want to see it for approval or suggested changes. Finally, the printer may want to use it as a guide in printing.

When the time arrives for embarking on the finished pictures, procedures become varied. Most illustrators finish the pictures one at a time; others start several and flit from one to the other, keeping a number of them in progress at the same time; some tackle their favorite compositions first while others horde them up until the home stretch. This is where temperament and experience dictate.

Theoretically, with composition, drawing and other factors worked out in preliminary sketches and clearly charted in the full-size *master* drawing, the final stage is one of technique, rendering what has been already completely planned. Sometimes things work out that way but there are always the imponderables. Can one maintain a fine creative edge throughout a long series? Can one guard one's time against ruinous interruptions? The physical and mental tides do not always flow consistently. Interest may flag toward the end of a long series. A problem of the conservation of creative energy faces the artist and only he can solve it, for it must be answered in terms of his own creative energy and temperament. Since the illustrator is harnessed to a definite delivery day, he has little or no time to spend waiting for a favorable mood. He usually is at his drawing board or easel, regardless of the inner weather And, all in all, this works out very well. No creative talent works completely smoothly and unremittingly. The hypochondriac artist who is constantly taking his creative temperature will soon have time for little else. The persistent worker has the advantage. There will be days when everything will be dropped in the wastebasket, but other days beginning with misgivings will end up in triumph.

As the series progresses toward completion, it is well to pause for comparisons and revaluations. Are the key characters who appear in picture after picture consistent? Do they seem to be the same person? Are the important accessories, machines, buildings, uniforms, boats and other objects correctly enough visualized to satisfy the sharp eyes of many children?

Finally, the finished drawings should be cleaned and protected with a paper flap. The captions with their page numbers should be written legibly on each drawing. If color separations are necessary, they should key with the necessary register marks, and the color swatches of the wanted colors should be painted in beside the drawing. A neat package of splendid drawings should be delivered on time.

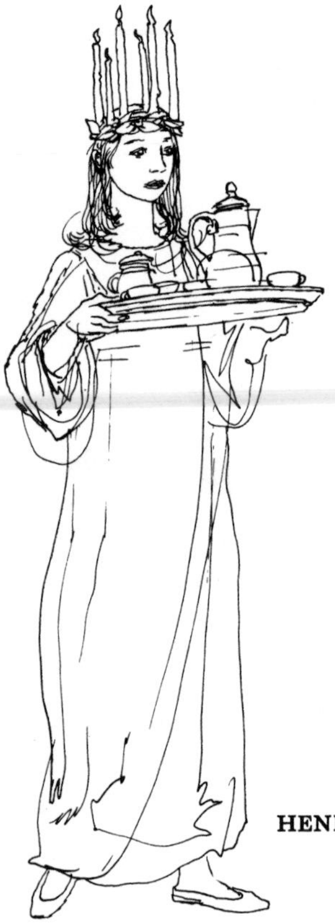

HENRY C. PITZ

192

EDWARD SOREL
King Carlo of Capri
Harcourt, Brace and Company

CHAPTER **16**

Getting Work

THE ARTIST ASPIRING TO WORK in the children's book field is usually a young person just out of art school; but whatever the age, ability or background, the question of getting established is the dominant one. Ninety-nine out of a hundred professionals have followed the same path in their novice days: they peddled their wares. Ever since publishers have needed illustrations, artists have been knocking at their doors with portfolios under their arms.

A personal interview, with a display of one's work, is the accustomed practice, but there are two other ways which we will mention and dispose of, for they are of minor value. One is to have an artist's agent who will take over the leg-work of selling talent. The agent is quite an important figure nowadays in the advertising and magazine fields but there are only a few who concern themselves with book illustration. The smaller fees do not attract them; their commission is usually twenty-five percent. Nor are they likely to be interested in the green artist unless the talent is exceptional. Although a competent agent could do a great deal to launch a promising talent, the artist would be deprived of a very valuable experience — the knowledge that comes from taking part in the give and take of publishing. Another method would be to prepare promotional material — cards, folders, photographs and reproductions of one's work — to be mailed out to possible clients. This could be a very valuable way of following up one's personal visits and keeping in touch with interested editors, but it is doubtful if any career has been launched by this method alone.

Personal visits are the traditional answer but they could be harmful if not carefully planned and thoughtfully prepared for. The stock in trade is one's portfolio of work. Personality counts for something but it is pictures that will elate or bore the editor.

A haphazard collection of pictures is of little value. Editors have decided ideas about the kind of pictures they can use and they quickly dismiss material that is remote from their own problems. It is the duty of the young artist to find out all that he or she possibly can about children's books, their needs, their message, their contents, their appeal, and their physical make-up. Long hours should be spent in the libraries and bookstores, not just idly leafing through the books that happen to suit the artist's taste but examining *everything*. The idea is to get some feeling of the entire field and not just a small corner of it. Notes should be taken of publishers' names, together with the kinds of books they produce, so that the climates or personalities of publishing firms will emerge. Then the artist is able to discern what to take where, and neither his own nor the editor's time will be wasted.

The bulk of the work should attempt to solve concrete problems in the children's book field. The problems could range from an age-old children's classic to an inventive tale that the artist or a friend has worked out. In the last case, an excellent idea would be to show a sketch dummy of the entire book with two or three of its illustrations finished to the limit of the artist's ability. It is well to show different types of book problems: jackets, end-papers and text illustrations. If the artist should have a few unusually good pieces that are not directly concerned with illustration, they may be included; but the run-of-the-mill type of art school problems such as regulation model studies, still-lifes, landscapes, wallpaper designs and acre-wide abstract "expressions" should be kept for other audiences. If there is anything of great value in any of these, it should be incorporated into the illustrative material shown.

PORTFOLIO PRESENTATION

Presentation is important. Even superlative drawings look better if tastefully and cleanly matted and mediocre things look less so. Presentation need go no further than cleaning up the borders of all draw-

194

ings or suitably matting them. Tidy paper flaps or cellophane will keep them fresh. They may be carried in the usual artist's portfolio or, if smaller, in the now popular sample books with transparent pages.

There is a point of balance between showing too few and too many items and this could be governed partly by the kind of illustrations shown. Less than seven or eight reasonably ambitious pieces may seem poverty-stricken, and more than fourteen or fifteen might be boring, particularly if they are much the same. Besides, it is wise to save something for a second or a third visit, for this is not a single battle but a campaign.

Drawings made for line reproduction (pen, brush, and ink) are portfolio staples. These are the kind of drawings that most beginners will be given to do for their first assignments. At least one of them should be designed for use, with one or more flat colors and the separations attached to the master drawing, to show the editor that the necessary know-how is present. Almost all novices prefer to work in full color and the best of these efforts should be included — but only the best. Full-color assignments are not likely to be given to beginners but full-color samples may contain an idea that could be translated into black and white.

The great majority of book publishers are concentrated in New York with a sprinkling in Philadelphia, Boston, and Chicago. The yellow pages of the telephone directories will furnish names and addresses. If the research in the libraries and bookstores has been well done, the aspirant will have some idea of the kind of things used by each publisher. The children's book editor in almost every case will be a woman and her assistants will also be women. One can travel from office to office, in the hope of finding an editor available or one can telephone and make an appointment. Editors are almost all uniformly kind and considerate, but very busy. They cannot be expected to give very much time to any one person; in fact, the aspirants are often screened first by an assistant. There is one large area for children's illustration that is often overlooked: the educational or text book field. A large proportion of this work is for children and their textbooks are usually lavishly illustrated. These are handled by a separate editorial staff, the educational editors.

The visits to editors should be done with some system and notes should be kept. When editors are interested, they will want your name and address. This information should be available on neatly printed cards. They may also want reproductions of some of your pictures for their files. The young artist seldom has photoengraving proofs of his work but he should have photographs or photostats made and sent promptly.

Great hopes should not be set upon the first visit. Not many are given work the first time. After all, there is a certain amount of chance in these visits. Not only must the work be of a kind and quality to be desired, but one must arrive when an assignment has become available. The first visit should be considered a preliminary exploration which will be followed by many others if the ground looks favorable.

Notes should be kept of these visits, and if an editor should suggest a return in a month or two, that should be complied with. Editors will almost never suggest a return unless they are interested.

The thought of continually making the rounds of publishers' offices may be distasteful to some. It is not as much fun as making pictures, but is a necessary part of the illustrator's education. He or she will have a lot of things to learn besides picturemaking; contacts with editors is not only necessary, but interesting and stimulating. It is the kind of apprenticeship that can pave the way to a long career of fruitful work.

After one has begun to do professional work, it is sometimes amazing what a potent publicity force one's reproduced work becomes. Book illustration is seen by other editors and, if it kindles their interest, they may wish to have the artist work for them. New assignments often come out of the blue, a reward not only for good work, but for the legwork to publishers that made possible the first assignments.

MARCIA BROWN
Once a Mouse
Charles Scribner's Sons

CHAPTER 17

The Field Today

LOOKING OUT INTO TODAY'S WORLD of children's illustrated books makes one blink and strain to comprehend the dazzle and scope of it. It is an empire now, busy and effervescent, drawing talent from sources never before tapped, bursting with ideas and ambitions, organized, competitive and highly competent. It has lost some of its sense of wonder; the amateur and tentative touch is gone and on the horizon is the threat of an over-confident professionalism. Pedantry did not disappear with the Victorian Age, nor sentimentality, although they take other guises. Moralizing and propaganda are still present, although they are not called that, because they are the moralizing and propaganda of our own time and inclination.

More books mean more dollars and we hope, more education, more delight and more awareness. If the writing, illustrations, and design of children's books is an art, it will not be obedient to push-button expansion. It will not be likely to flower under clinical eyes and automation techniques.

The field has been remarkably fortunate in the people it has drawn to it. Its writers, artists, editors and librarians come from the same imperfect stock that inhabits the rest of the globe, but all in all they can be counted upon for a vocational devotion greater than most, an allegiance to a sector of human activity they believe in and love, and an unusual endowment of brains and talent. The financial rewards for this devoted company have tended to be modest, so the field has not tempted the fortune hunters. But publishers' profits have taken wings in many cases, and little has been done to share these with those who have made success possible. The excellence of today's children's books has come to pass because of the lavish care and anxious affection of a body of talented and concerned individuals, and if giantism overtakes them it may perform its usual magic of changing individuals into cogs.

But today's children's books are an achievement — something we can be proud of. Many countries, chiefly those of Western Europe, have and are producing works of high excellence; others with limited publishing facilities are struggling, improving and satisfying their growing appetites by importations from the more prolific countries. Conditions have conspired to give the United States, however, not only an enormous advantage in volume but an allover superiority in design and execution. Our best books are no better than the best of other countries, but there are more of them. Our average is higher. With allowances made for the many — too many — weaknesses in American production, the total impression is of strength, variety, inventiveness, and competence. Future observers may look back and call ours a "golden age" of children's bookmaking.

BETH AND JOSEPH KRUSH
Coarse Gold Gulch
Doubleday and Company, Inc.

It would be easy to expect large volume from our great population and high degree of industrialization. The excellent quality of so much of our writing, design and illustration might be less predictable; but there is an eagerness in the land to write and make pictures, and the writer and artist are no longer oddities. In fact, they have taken on glamour in most people's eyes. Besides, there is both stability and ferment in our large population and a rich diversity of racial strains. It is a good background for the recruiting of talent for the book arts.

In addition to our rich pool of native talent, is the fertilizing effect of so many foreign talents that have adopted us. They come to us because we promise a freer life, opportunity and an ample livelihood. Besides this, we publish the work of many foreign artists and introduce them to our large public. Our alert and sharp-eyed editors now have a regular practice of scanning the foreign fields and buying the American rights for some of the finest foreign work. So, by and large, American children are seeing the best illustration that the world has to offer.

In return, some of our best books are translated and sold abroad, so that one can have the experience of searching the foreign book-stores for finely illustrated books and being offered the foreign edition of a book that has already appeared at home. But our poorest books are exported also; the cheap comic sheets and the gaudy, badly printed, and atrociously pictured board-bound books designed for the discount and *five and ten* markets. We may deplore this, for it shows others our discreditable side, but we have not forced these things on the foreign reprint houses; they buy them to satisfy a hunger in their own countries. It can be said with considerable truth that the American publishers supply the home public with much of the best foreign material and little that is poor, while the foreign market takes from us much of our worst.

JOSEPH LOW
Mother Goose
Riddle Rhymes
Harcourt, Brace and Company

JAN LE WITT
The Vegatabull
Harcourt, Brace and Company

Within the past two decades, the sense of competition among our publishers of children's books has intensified. They have discovered what a gold mine a children's book department can be and, in certain cases, it has saved the year's figures from going into the red. So there is more snap and crackle, and more tension in the editorial offices of the children's book departments than there used to be. The search for variety has been very fruitful but sometimes it becomes a scamper after mere novelty. The bizarre and extreme modes of contemporary art, the inept and clumsy, disguised under the name of modernism, the trivialities of the latest, *chic* fad have had their innings and there are signs that they are fading. Too often the stuffiness of the old has merely been replaced by the inconsequence of the new. But the mistakes and failures can be brushed to one side, and we can count our blessings for the yearly bulk of creditable books. Never have so many handsome and worthwhile books been offered to the young of any nation.

GERALD ROSE
Old Winkle and the Seagulls
Faber and Faber

LYLE JUSTIS
Unpublished Illustration

JANICE HOLLAND
Christopher Goes to the Castle
Charles Scribner's Sons

The young artist who is ambitious to become part of this world has the odds on his side if he has something to offer. Intelligence, earnestness and a genuine impulse to belong to it can be the foundation. On this can be built the gifts which talent bestows, and accumulated *know-how* that time and experience should bring. The children's book world is not fenced in. The powers that rule it are dispersed and not despotic. They are used to and expect young blood to be pushing in. This is not to say that the young artist will be immediately embraced and made a member of the fold. Occasionally this happens, but usually the novice is treated kindly and if his pictures are worthy he is invited to come back. If he is persistent enough to return for a second, third, or fourth visit with fresh material of excellence, one or more editors will begin to feel that he is worth a trial.

With the first hurdle passed, the artist may have begun a lifetime career. The book field is less at the mercy of fad and fancy than the magazine and advertising fields. The better illustrators tend to become institutions, serving generation after generation of young minds. So the children's artists are both young and old and in between. Perhaps it might be better to describe them as young artists of all ages.

No one knows if there is a saturation point for children's books. Children's appetites for texts and pictures have grown from year to year; parents' and relatives' pockets have grown too, so the future seems to promise more children, more dollars, and more books. We have become so accustomed to the experience of constant growth and expansion that we almost believe it to be preordained. A change in the economic climate could alter all this but regardless of whether we print more or fewer books, it is vastly more important that they be beautiful than merely numerous. In the midst of congratulating ourselves on the large number of superior children's books we produce every year, we will be laying plans to surpass ourselves in beauty and quality.

HENRY C. PITZ

203

Bibliography

BLAND, DAVID, THE ILLUSTRATION OF BOOKS, London: Faber & Faber, 1951.

BLAND, DAVID, A HISTORY OF BOOK ILLUSTRATION, New York: World Publishing Co., 1958.
> The only comprehensive history of the entire field of book illustration in English. Packed with information and an invaluable reference book.

COLBY, JEAN POINDEXTER, THE CHILDREN'S BOOK FIELD, New York: Pellegrini and Cudahy, 1952.

COOKE, DONALD, COLOR BY OVERPRINTING, Philadelphia: Winston, 1955.

DARTON, FREDERICK J. H., CHILDREN'S BOOKS IN ENGLAND, Cambridge: Cambridge University Press, 1958.

DOBSON, AUSTIN, THOMAS BEWICK AND HIS PUPILS, London: Chatto & Windus, 1884.

ELLIS, RICHARD, BOOK ILLUSTRATION, Kingsport: Kingsport Press, 1952.

GAVAULT, PAUL, LES LIVRES de L'ENFANCE du XVe au XIXe Siècle, Two Volumes. Paris: Gumucheau & Cie, N. D.

HAMILTON, SINCLAIR, EARLY AMERICAN BOOK ILLUSTRATORS AND WOOD ENGRAVERS, Princeton: Princeton University Library Chronicle, 1958.

LEHMANN-HAUPT, HELLMUT, THE BOOK IN AMERICA, New York: R. R. Bowker Company, 1951.

LEWIS, JOHN, A HANDBOOK OF TYPE AND ILLUSTRATION, London: Faber & Faber, 1956.

MAHONY, BERTHA E.; LATIMER, LOUISE PAYSON; FOLMSBEE, BEULAH, ILLUSTRATORS OF CHILDREN'S BOOKS, 1744-1945, Boston: The Horn Book, 1946.

MILLER, BERTHA MAHONY; VIGUERS, RUTH HILL; DALPHIN, MARCIA, ILLUSTRATORS OF CHILDREN'S BOOKS, 1946-1956, Boston: The Horn Book, 1958.
> These two books are mines of information about the illustration of children's books. There are short biographies and bibliographies of all the important illustrators of the past and present. Compiled for the American point of view but containing material about many European artists.

MOORE, ANNE CARROLL, THE ART OF BEATRIX POTTER, London and New York: Frederick Warne & Co., 1958.

MUIR, PERCY, ENGLISH CHILDREN'S BOOKS, 1600-1900, London: B. T. Batsford Ltd., 1954.

MYRICK, FRANK B., A PRIMER IN BOOK PRODUCTION, New York: Bookbinding and Book Production, 1945.

PITZ, HENRY C. A TREASURY OF AMERICAN BOOK ILLUSTRATION, New York: Watson-Guptill Publications and American Studio Books, 1947.

PITZ, HENRY C., THE PRACTICE OF ILLUSTRATION, New York: Watson-Guptill Publications, 1947.

ROSENBACH, ABRAHAM SIMON WOLF, EARLY AMERICAN CHILDREN'S BOOKS, Portland, Maine: Southworth Press, 1933.

ROSNER, CHARLES, THE GROWTH OF THE BOOK JACKET, London: Sylvan Press Limited, 1954.

SMITH, JANET ADAM, CHILDREN'S ILLUSTRATED BOOKS, London: Collins, 1948.

TEDESCO, A. P., THE RELATIONSHIP BETWEEN TYPE AND ILLUSTRATION, New York: George McKillin & Son, n. d.

TUER, ANDREW W. FORGOTTEN CHILDREN'S BOOKS, London: The Leadenhall Press, Ltd., 1898-9.

WHITE, GLEESON, CHILDREN'S BOOKS AND THEIR ILLUSTRATORS, New York: The Studio Limited, 1897-8.

Index

Action, capturing of, 110; see also Sketching
Aesop's Fables, 20, 45; illus. from, 21
Age groups, requirements of, 106-110, 148
Alice's Adventures in Wonderland, 36-38, 101
Anderson, Alexander, 62-63
Anderson, Hans Christian, 51, 54, 101
Angelo, Valenti, 88; illus. by, 85
Ardizzone, Edward, 46, 47, 92
Artzybasheff, Boris, 90; illus. by, 85
Awards, 88

Bauer, John, 59
Bawden, Edward, 46, 48; illus. by, 46, 154
Ben-Day screens, 176
Bewick, Thomas, 26, 29-30, 33, 62-63
Blake, William, 26-28
Bleeds, 138, 140, 146, 165-166
Blegvad, Erik, illus. by, 102, 157, 182
Blind stamping, 140
Bourges sheets, 175
Brown, Marcia, illus. by, 142, 144, 197
Brunhoff, Jean de, 56
Busch, Wilhelm, 53

Caldecott, Randolph, 38, 40-41, 42, 46, 88
Cady, Walter Harrison, 80
Carroll, Lewis, 36, 38, 42
Chapbooks, 23-24
Chappell, Warren, illus. by, 143, 149
Chopping, Richard, 48
Collotype, 158, 163
Color, reproduction of, 169-182;
    see also Groups; Reproduction
Comenius, Bishop, 19-20
Cox, Palmer, 80-81
Crane, Walter, 38-41
Cruikshank, George, 31-33

Darley, Felix Octavius, 64-66
Denslow, W. W., illus. by, 184
Details in illustration, 108, 192; see also Sketching
Direct reproduction, 157-164 *passim,* 178
Disney, Walt, illus. by, 114
Doré, Paul Gustave, 55-56
Double pages, 146, 148; see also Bleeds
Doyle, Richard, 33; illus. by, 35
Drawing for reproduction, 165-182 *passim*
Dugan, William, illus. by, 115, 134
Dulac, Edmund, 42-45, 86
Dummy, preparation of, 188-191
Duvoisin, Roger, 89, 98, illus. by, 97, 141

Editors, contacting of, 193-196
Education of illustrators, 98, 105-110
Endpapers, design of, 141-142
Engraving, 158-162, 175; see also Line cut
Enlargement of illustration, 166-168
Etching, 27-28, 160-161; see also Line cut

Falls, Charles B., 82-83
Final drawings, preparation of, 191-192, 194-195;
    see also Reproduction; Sketching
Floethe, Richard, 58, illus. by, 93
Formats, see Layout
Frasconi, Antonio, 94-95
Fraser, Claud Lovat, 45
Frequency of illustrations, 135-150, 188
Freund, Rudolf, 88, 94; illus. by, 132, 183
Frontispiece, design of, 143-145
Frost, Arthur B., 66, 75-76, 78, 80; illus. by, 75-77

Gabler, Grace, 48, 49
Gergely, Tibor, 91; illus. by, 112-113
Gerhard, Mae, illus. by, 79, 129, 134
Grahame, Kenneth, 46, 72; see also
    Wind in the Willows, The
Greenaway, Kate, 38, 40-41, 42
Grimm, The Brothers (Jakob and Wilhelm) 31, 51,
    54, 101; illus. from, 144

Halftones, introduction of, 68-69, 82; reproduction
    of, 158-161, 176, 178-180
Harris, Joel Chandler, 76, 77
Hassall, Joan, 45
Hoffmann-Donner, Dr. Heinrich, 52
Homer, Winslow, 66; illus. by, 64
Houghton, Arthur Boyd, 34, 35
Indirect reproduction, 157-164 *passim;*
    see also Reproduction
Intaglio, 158, 162

Jacket design, 136-139

Kemble, Edward W., 66, 76, 78
Knight, Hilary, illus. by, 104-105, 111
Krush, Beth and Joseph, 91, 92; illus. by, 13,
    198-199

Laite, Gordon, illus. by, 126, 130
Layout, 90, 135-150 *passim,* 166-168, 188-191
Lear, Edward, 36, 53; illus. by, 36, 37
Leech, John, 32, 33
Legrand, Edy, 56, 96; illus. by, 57
Length of books, 106-109, 135-136
Light box, use of, 174-175
Line cut, reproduction of, 158-160, 169-175,
    177-178, 195; use of, 27-28, 82

Linoleum cut, 94, 158-160
Lithography, 52, 163-164, 176-178
Low, Joseph, 94; illus. by, 15, 142, 151, 200

MacDonald, George, 34, 54
Märchen, see Grimm, The Brothers
McNaught, Harry, 91; illus. by, 133
Medals, 88
Milhous, Katherine, 98; illus. by, 84
Miller, J. P. illus. by, 96, 116, 155
Monvel, Boutet de, 56, 57
Mordvinoff, Nicolas, 89, 92; illus. by, 92, 127
Muir, Percy H., 5, 25, 38

Newbery, John, 25, 62, 88
Nicholson, William, 41
Nielsen, Kay, 54

Offset printing, 164; see also Lithography
Overlapping, see Halftones, reproduction of
Overlays, see Separations

Papers, see Separations
Pen drawings, 68, 82, 94, 140; see also Line cuts
Perrault, Charles, 51; illus. from books by, 31, 32, 143
Photoengraving, introduction of, 41, 68-70, 157; reproduction by, 158-164, 173; see also Separations
Pierce, Leona, 94; illus. by, 94, 139
Pitz, Henry C., illus. by, 89, 147, 171, 189, 190, 192, 203
Potter, Beatrix, 42, 98; illus. by, 43
Printing, see Reproduction
Provensen, Alice and Martin, 91, 96; illus. by, 2, 122-123
Publishers, location of, 195
Punch, 32, 33, 38
Pyle, Howard, 54, 66-74, 78, 82, 98, 101; illus. by, 66, 67, 69, 70, 74

Quality of book design, 100-102, 197-203, and *passim*

Rackham, Arthur, 42, 86; illus. by, 43
Raverat, Gwen, 45
Reduction of illustrations, 166-168
Relief-etching, 27-28; see also Line cut
Relief printing, method of, 158-161; see also Reproduction
Remington, Frederic, 78; illus. by, 77
Reproduction, 136, 140; methods of, 157-164; preparations for, 165-182; see also Halftones; Line cut; Linoleum cut; Lithography; Photo-engraving; Relief-etching; Woodblocks

Richter, Ludwig, 53; illus. by, 51, 53
Robinson Crusoe, 31, 54, 55, 101; illus. from, 71
Rojankovsky, Feodor, 56, 89, 90; illus. by, 14, 91, 124-125, 145
Rose, Gerald, 48; illus. by, 137, 187, 201

Schoonover, Frank, 72; illus. by, 71
Searle, Ronald, 47
Separations, making of, 171-182, 192
Shenton, Edward, 96; illus. by, 84
Shepard, Ernest H., 46
Signatures, 135-136, 191
Silk-screen, see Surface printing
Size of illustration, 106-107, 135-150 *passim,* 166-168
Sketching, 110, 146, 188-191
Smith, Jesse Willcox, 72
Snyder, Jerome, illus. by, 12, 165
Sorel, Edward, illus. by, 19, 120, 193
Spine of book, see Jacket design
Spot illustration, 143, 144
Struwwelpeter, 52, 101
Surface printing, 158, 163-164; see also Lithography

Tail-piece, use of, 150
Tegner, Hans, 54
Tenggren, Gustaf, 89, 90; illus. by, 17, 91, 121
Tenniel, John, 38; illus. by, 37
Thomson, Hugh, 41
Thornycroft, Priscilla, 48; illus. by, 50
Tipping in, 90
Title page, design of, 143-145
Tracing, 188; see also Separations
Transparencies, see Separations
Trnka, Jire, 60
Type size, choice of, 108, 138-139, 143, 144, 151-154

Uncle Remus, 75-77

Ward, Lynd, 84; illus. by, 86
Weisgard, Leonard, 92; illus. by, 93, 135
White-line technique, 29-30, 33; see also Bewick, Thomas
Wilson, Edward A., 72-74
Wilson, Maurice, 48, 49
Wind in the Willows, The, 101; illus. from, 46
Wirth-Miller, Dennis, 48
Wonderful Wizard of Oz, The, 101; illus. from, 184
Woodcuts, use of, 19-26, 83, 94, 158-160; examples of, 24 and *passim*
Wyeth, N. C., 72, 74; illus. by, 71

Zimnik, Reiner, 59, 98; illus. by, 16, 58, 99